Joy in the
Journey

Encouragement for
Homeschooling Moms

Joy in the Journey

Encouragement for Homeschooling Moms

Lori Hatcher

Joy in the Journey: Encouragement for Homeschooling Moms

Copyright © 2012 by Lori Hatcher

Manufactured in the USA
Printed by Lulu Enterprises, Inc.
http://www.lulu.com

860 Aviation Parkway
Suite 300
Morrisville, NC 27560

First Printing: March 2012

International Standard Book Number: 979-1-105-35503-5

Book and Cover Design: Grant Tucker

Cover Photo by Leigh Essig
www.essigphotography.com
Special Thanks to the Brad & Melissa Bird family

For more words of encouragement and inspiration, please visit Lori's blog at
http://www.lori-benotweary.blogspot.com.

This book is dedicated to Cindy and Elizabeth Kay,
sisters who have gone on before.

Contents

ACKNOWLEDGEMENTS

Above all, praise, honor, and glory for this book belong to God, its true Author. Through every step of the process, He directed my path.

Thanks also go to the precious members of my homeschool group, Forest Acres Christian Educators. You believed in the value of my writing before I did. You were the ones who said, "You should write a book someday." Thank you for believing in me.

I am thankful to Lisa, who attended my first Christian Devotions Writers' Conference with me. It was there the idea for this book was born.

I am also thankful for all of you who have prayed this book into existence. Mandy, Sandy, Alicia, Susie, Debbie, my dear Ladies' Bible Study friends, and my Power of a Praying Parent group, you are amazing. Mom, Dad, and Tina, I love you!

I am thankful for the members of the Palmetto Christian Writers' Network who provided the practical advice I needed to move through the publication process. Jana Daley, godly homeschooling mom and friend, caught the vision early for *Joy in the Journey* and provided invaluable editing assistance and encouragement. Mitch Smith, a homeschooling father and business man with a heart to enable homeschooling families to succeed moved the book from my heart to your hands.

And where would I be without the precious daughters God gave me? Kristen and Mary Leigh, what a privilege it is to be your mom and to have been your homeschool teacher. Homeschooling was certainly a group effort -- while I was educating you, God was educating me. I trust we all received a great education. I love you so much!

Finally, I would like to thank my amazing husband, David. You have supported me in so many ways. One of the greatest gifts you gave me was the privilege of staying home and rearing our daughters. You chose to invest your treasure in our children rather than in a big house or a new car. You worked long hours so I could stay home with them, and I am profoundly grateful.

My hope is that *Joy in the Journey* will encourage homeschooling mothers everywhere to "be not weary in well doing, for you will reap a harvest if you do not faint." (Galatians 6:9)

To God be the glory!

TO THE READER

This book contains God's words of encouragement to you. It is a compilation of devotions written during the ten years I served as support group leader of our local homeschool group, Forest Acres Christian Educators (FACE) in Columbia, South Carolina. As I wrote each devotional, I asked God to give me the words of hope and empowerment women need to successfully homeschool.

As a 17-year veteran home educator, each devotion reflects what God taught me as I homeschooled my children. I pray the lessons I share will be ones that will bless you. Application questions and an action step after each reading will help you apply the lessons to your own unique life situation. This book may be useful as a weekly devotional or for use with a support group. The topics are suitable as discussion starters or themes for entire meetings.

May God richly bless you as you seek to honor Him!

For more words of encouragement and inspiration, please visit my blog at **http://www.lori-benotweary.blogspot.com.**

August

THE HARDEST THING I'VE EVER DONE

" I can do all things through CHRIST who gives me strength."
Philippians 4:13

I thought my college Head and Neck Anatomy class was hard. I thought studying for and passing the National Board for Dental Hygiene, all seven hours of it, was hard, too. I thought working full time and volunteering at church was hard. I thought childbirth was hard -- and colic, months of colic. It was hard to surrender my child over for surgery at nine months old. So was praying for her salvation since before she was born. Acting in front of 13,000 people was hard. Staying married during rough times is always hard.

In comparison though, homeschooling remains the hardest thing I've ever done. And if I had the choice to make again, I'd do it in a heartbeat.

Despite the lonely days when I thought if I didn't see another human being over three feet tall I would scream. Despite the 547 days of phonics instruction before one of my daughters could read a four-word sentence without pausing. Despite the buckets of tears we shed over Chemistry, Algebra, and Geometry. Despite the days when fear would grip me as I wondered if I might be single-handedly sabotaging my children's entire academic future. Despite the days when I dealt with the same sin for the 100th time, and then had to correct it in my children as well.

If I had the choice to make again, I'd do it in a heartbeat.

I would do it for the joy of hearing my daughter pray to receive Christ into her heart during morning devotions. I would do it for the pleasure of watching her read all the way through *Go Dog Go*, knowing I had taught her to read. I would do it again for the character training I received throughout the years. I would do it again for the opportunity to trust God when I knew that apart from His work in our homeschool, it would not succeed.

I would do it again for the privilege of watching Him work in each daughter's life as she came to understand the world through a Christian perspective. I would do it again for the precious gift of time . . . never enough, but SO much more than many of my friends had with their children during their growing up years. I would do it again for every field trip vacation we took to fascinating places on a shoestring budget. I would do it again for the chance to pray and ask God for all we needed and see Him provide bountifully. I would do it again so I could own part of my daughters' high school graduations and college acceptances. I would do it again for the satisfaction of knowing I had obeyed what God told me to do.

If I had the choice to make again, I'd do it in a heartbeat.

Application Questions

1. What are some hard things you have done in your lifetime? Were the results worth the effort?
2. What character qualities did God develop in you through the challenges of persevering despite difficulty? Are you better for having persevered?
3. What do you hope to accomplish by homeschooling your child(ren)?

Action Step for This Week

With your husband, write a brief philosophy of education. It doesn't have to be long or complicated; simply write down why you are homeschooling and what you hope to accomplish. Use this as a plumb line for the decisions you will make concerning curriculum, activities, and ministries this school year.

Prayer of Commitment

Lord Jesus, more than anything else, I want to be faithful to the calling you have placed on my life to homeschool my child(ren). While I know we may experience challenging days, months, and even years, I also believe by faith you will do wonderful things in and through our family's homeschooling journey. Give my husband and me the wisdom and courage to embrace this opportunity to raise our children in the nurture and admonition of You. Help us remember that apart from You, we can do nothing, but with you, we can do all things.

AUGUST

CHOOSING THE ROAD LESS TRAVELED

"And let us not be weary in well doing: for in due season we shall reap, if we faint not."
Galatians 6:9

Robert Frost wrote, "Two roads diverged in a wood and I, I took the one less traveled by, and that has made all the difference." As homeschooling parents, you have chosen a road less travelled. As you begin your school year, may I commend you for choosing to educate your children at home. You have not chosen an easy path, but you are following one chosen by the ancients. Deuteronomy 6:6-7 says this, "These commandments that I give you today are to be on your hearts. Impress them upon your children. Talk about them when you sit at home, when you lie down, and when you get up." This is the essence of Christian parenting, and the essence of home-schooling. You have chosen a good and noble calling, but you will not accomplish it without sacrifice.

Instead of orderly ladies' Bible studies after the children go to school, you have chosen to act out the story of David and Goliath on your hands and knees in the living room with your five-year old. Instead of enjoying a leisurely cup of espresso at the bookstore with a girlfriend, you have chosen to enjoy apple juice and Little Debbie cakes in between phonics lessons and science. Instead of emotionally detached intellectual debates over the proper methods of rearing the next generation of young people, you have chosen to discipline a young one for disobedience and then hold him while he cries.

Instead of living in a house that stays clean all day because no one is home, you have chosen to live in one where books are everywhere and phone messages are written in crayon because it is the only writing implement available. Instead of delegating the job to a "professional," you have chosen to be there when the first book is read, when the light bulb goes off in multiplication, and when the tadpole finally grows legs and becomes a frog.

Homeschooling mother, know that you are investing in eternity as you devote your time and energy to homeschool your children. You have them for such a short time, and there is much to learn.

Application Questions

1. What are some spiritual goals you would like to accomplish with each of your children this school year?
2. How can you incorporate spiritual lessons into the day to day routine of life?

Action Step for This Week

Ask God to show you areas of spiritual growth that need to take place in your children and yourself this school year. As He reveals these things to you, write them down and keep the list somewhere safe. Pray over these areas and commit them to God.

Prayer of Commitment

Lord, it is my heart's desire to rear my children to love and follow You. I know You have called me to this task, but sometimes I am discontent when I look around at other mothers who seem to have an easier, more glamorous life. Help me remember that while I may not see all of the results in my children immediately, next week, or even next year, I can trust Your word which tells me that I will reap a harvest if I do not faint. Help me seek first your kingdom, both for me and for my family. When I start to grumble, remind me of the great privilege it is to stay home with my children and raise them in the nurture and admonition of the Lord. Remind me, in everything, to give thanks.

AUGUST

WHEN YOU'VE LOST YOUR JOY

"Do you not know? Have you not heard? The Lord is the everlasting God the Creator of the ends of the earth. He will not grow tired or weary, and His understanding no one can fathom. He gives strength to the weary and increases the power of the weak. Even youths grow tired and fall; but those who hope in the Lord will renew their strength. They will soar on wings like eagles; they will run and not grow weary, they will walk and not faint."

Isaiah 40:28-31

Do you remember your first day of school? You had brand new clothes, new pencils and notebooks, and the mysterious, unknown teacher to face. Depending on past experiences, you might have been eagerly anticipating the beginning of school, or your heart might have been heavy with anxiety or fear of what the new school year would bring.

Homeschooling is not really that different. Now though, we anticipate the first day of school as a parent/teacher, not as a student. Depending on past experience, you might be eagerly anticipating the beginning of a new school year, or you might be filled with dread, wondering what the year will hold.

In my early years of homeschooling, I often fell into the first category. Naïve in my understanding and self-confident in the fact that I was smarter than my students, I couldn't wait to tackle simple addition and first grade spelling. I would find myself weary by the end of the school year, but after a few weeks of summer vacation, a few "mommy" novels, (i.e. those with words containing more than short vowel sounds), and a new Sonlight catalog, I was recharged and eager to plan for the new school year.

I remember the first summer I wasn't eager to begin. As the new school year approached, I felt a sense of dread and loss rather than enthusiasm. The realization had dawned on me that homeschooling was hard work, I was not always smarter than my students, and I didn't always see the stellar academic performances I had expected. I never questioned our commitment to homeschool, but I was less than enthusiastic about beginning a new school year. I also knew that without joy and enthusiasm on my part, our homeschool year would not begin well.

One morning during my quiet time, I was especially burdened by the knowledge that I was not looking forward to the beginning of school. I decided to talk with the Lord about it.

"Lord, right now I'm not too excited about beginning school. I look around at the novels I haven't read, the naps I haven't taken, and the summer projects I haven't completed. I can't bear to think of opening those school books and planning for a new year. I really do love homeschooling, and I wouldn't choose any other way, but right now, I'm just not very enthusiastic. I can't muster it up within myself, so I'm going to need You to give it to me. Would you please, and hurry?

I was praying based on the promise of God in Psalm 37:4 that says that He will give us the desires of our hearts. He doesn't promise to give us everything our heart desires, but He will give us the desires our hearts should have.

Before too many days of praying for enthusiasm, God gave it to me. How sweet it was to begin a new homeschooling year knowing that God had given me the precious gift of excitement for the task He had ordained for me to do. I encourage you, dear sister, if you are dreading the beginning of the school year, ask our Father to give you joy to tackle the job ahead, and watch what He will do in your own heart.

Application Questions
1. How do you feel about beginning a new homeschooling year?
2. Do you need to ask God to give you energy and enthusiasm to begin the year on a positive note?

Action Step for This Week
If you lack enthusiasm for the new school year, pray and ask God to fill your heart with His joy, peace, and energy.

Prayer of Commitment

Lord, thank You for the privilege of homeschooling my children. As the new school year begins, please fill my heart with energy and enthusiasm for the year that lies ahead. Help me set a positive tone in our household. Equip and enable me to do the work You have called me to do, and help this to be the best homeschooling year yet.

THE MERCY PLANT

"His mercies fail not. They are new every morning. Great is Your faithfulness."

Lamentations: 3:22-23

I call it my Mercy Plant. It has bloomed in my side yard for the last three years. Its formal name is Mexican Petunia, but from the very first morning, I have called the Mercy Plant. Long, slender fronds of dark green leaves sprout deep purple flowers every morning. Sometimes I pass the plant at four-thirty or five a.m. when I let the dog out. No matter how early I emerge, the flowers are there, open, awaiting the morning. By three-thirty or four in the afternoon, each flower will have launched itself off its stem in a parachute flight to the ground.

By the next morning, new flowers appear, and the cycle begins again. Every morning they burst into bloom; every afternoon they lie spent on the ground. I call it the Mercy Plant because it reminds me of Lamentations 3:22-23, "His mercies fail not. They are new every morning. Great is Your faithfulness."

Perhaps you had a terrific year of homeschooling last year. The children were eager learners. You were patient and organized. You scheduled appropriate field trips and took time out for service projects and visits to elderly. You are eagerly anticipating the new school year and can't wait to get started. God bless you! You need to read on.

Perhaps your school year wasn't perfect. Maybe it didn't even come close. You started out organized, but it went downhill fast. The children were behind in their lessons, your only field trip was an occasional stop at the grocery store, and elderly people run (walk) the other way when they see your kids coming. You know the Lord wants you to homeschool, but you haven't been able to muster up much enthusiasm or creativity for the new year.

The message of the Mercy Plant is for you. "His mercies fail not. They are new every morning. Great is thy faithfulness." Today is a new day, filled with God's grace and mercy toward you. This school year is a new school year, filled with fresh opportunities, second chances, and new beginnings. It stands on its own, but you don't have to. I encourage you to ponder the lessons you learned from last year, and then put that year behind you. Turn your face toward the new year, and ask God to inspire, encourage, and equip you.

Thank God for the privilege of homeschooling. Rest in God's mercy day by day, knowing that like the Mercy flowers, what He gives you will be spent by the end of the day, but each morning He will send you new mercies...and you can't wake up earlier than God! Remember the words of the Apostle Paul, "Forgetting those things which are behind, I press toward the mark of the high calling of God in Christ Jesus." (*Philippians 3:16*) My prayers are with you as you begin your new school year in light of God's mercy.

Application Questions

1. When you think back to last school year, what aspect of it most needs the hope of God's mercy?
2. How should God's merciful nature affect how you homeschool this year?
3. What is the balance in accepting God's mercy when your efforts fall short and using God's mercy as an excuse not to be diligent and responsible with your homeschooling?

Action Step for This Week

Commit, by God's mercy to put the past behind you and embrace the new school year as a brand new chance to honor and glorify Him.

Prayer of Commitment

Lord, whether last year was a good one or not, You have granted me a fresh start this school year. Enable and equip me to be the best homeschooling mother I can be. Help me give You the glory when things go well and rest in Your mercy when they don't. Remind me to extend the same mercy and grace You show toward me to those around me. Use each experience of this year to draw us all into a closer walk with You as we trust You day by day for new mercies.

September

HOMESCHOOLING IS A SPIRITUAL ENDEAVOR

DADDY'S BOOK

HOW DO YOU USE YOUR WORDS?

THE DAY GOD SHOWED UP

HOMESCHOOLING IS A SPIRITUAL ENDEAVOR

"Come unto me, all you who are weary and heavy laden, and I will give you rest."
Matthew 11:28

"The purpose of the voice of condemnation is to push you away from His presence -- that which is the very source of your victory. The purpose of the voice of conviction is to press you into the face of Christ."
Bob Sorge, *Secrets of the Secret Place* (Oasis House)

Sometimes I forget that homeschooling is a spiritual endeavor. I forget that it is only through the empowering and equipping of God's Spirit that I have any hope of success. Somehow, though I know it to be true, that I can do all things through Christ Who strengthens me, I sometimes begin my day without a moment spent in His presence. Brushing Him breezily aside, I dive into my busy day without taking even a moment to consult with Him. I wonder, how many of the "imperative" items on my to-do list might be cast aside if I had held them up to His wise eyes? Better yet, if I sat before Him with an empty page and asked, "Lord, what would you have me to do today?" how different would my to-do list be?

It is no wonder then, when I fail miserably, the voice of the enemy shouts loud words of condemnation into my ear. The voice of the enemy causes feelings of failure, doubt, confusion, and defeat. The voice pushes me away from the things that are good and right. The voice of Satan isolates me from those fellow sojourners whom God has placed alongside to help me. His voice makes me doubt whether I have a right to an audience with the King Whose presence I have neglected so many times.

But God the Father is long suffering and forgiving, slow to anger and abounding in love. (Exodus 34:6) He forgets my sin of independence as quickly as I confess it, and He runs to take me in His arms and restore me to a right relationship with Him. Do you realize that the only time scripture reveals God hurrying is when He, as the waiting and watching Father, runs to welcome His prodigal home?

Dear sister, whether you are enjoying success or are experiencing struggles, I encourage you to begin each day with an appointment with God. As you seek Him through prayer and His word, He will give you wisdom (James 1:5), strength (Philippians 4:13), freedom from fear and anxiety (Philippians 4:6), and clear direction for each day (Isaiah 30:21).

Even 15 minutes with the Savior each morning is an investment in the quality and effectiveness of your day, of your very life! Time spent at Jesus' feet is never time wasted. Best of all, if your heart and mind are filled with His words, when the accuser whispers lies in to your ears, you will recognize whom it is that is speaking. Homeschooling mom, run to Jesus!

Application Questions

1. Do you tend to view your family's homeschooling as an academic endeavor or a spiritual one?
2. If you view it as an academic one, are you missing out by not inviting God's power into your day?
3. If you view it as a spiritual one, do you still have a tendency to homeschool in your own strength?
4. How can you access God's power during the day to enable and equip you for the task of homeschooling?

Action Step for This Week

Write into your lesson plan a "quiet time" for all members of your family as the first part of your school day. If you have young children, you can teach them to sit quietly with their Bibles for 15 minutes. Even a toddler can look through a picture Bible and pray a simple prayer.

Prayer of Commitment

Lord, I know that 'apart from You, I can do nothing,' (John 15:5) but sometimes I don't act like it. I charge through my day and my to-do list without a glance Your way. I am so thankful that when I fail, You are there to gently remind me that You want to help me. Your 'yoke is easy and Your burden is light' when I operate within Your strength. Help me seek You first in the morning, and train my children to establish the habit of a daily quiet time.

DADDY'S BOOK

"This book of the law shall not depart out of your mouth; but you shall meditate therein day and night, that you may observe to do according to all that is written therein: for then you shall make your way prosperous, and then you shall have good success."
Joshua 1:8

It was my first summer away from home, and my father wanted to be sure I stayed close to the Lord. Daddy was always reading the latest devotional book, so before I left, he presented one to me. "Will you promise me that you'll read it every day?" I rolled my eyes and sighed a bit, "Yes, Dad, I'll read it." I tucked it into my already too-full suitcase and wondered what important item I was going to have to leave behind to make room for Dad's book.

The weeks flew by, and I occasionally thought about the book, usually after I was already in bed and too tired to pull it out of the suitcase where it had remained since my arrival. It was a full summer, with lots to do see. I especially enjoyed having a room to myself with a television – a luxury I had not had at home. There were so many shows to choose from that I could watch something different every night when I wasn't out with my friends, or taking in some of the local events.

Before I realized it, the summer was over and it was time to return home. As much as I had enjoyed the freedom of living on my own and working my first "real" job, I had missed my family too. It was so good to see them again! As they gathered around to hear my stories, I plundered my suitcase looking for the souvenirs I had carefully chosen for each of them. Dad's eyes scanned the suitcase's contents and his eyes fell on the devotional book he had sent with me.

"How did you enjoy reading it?" he asked as he opened the book to the first chapter. Before I could answer, a note fell out. It was written in my dad's handwriting and contained words of love and affirmation to me. Then a second piece of paper fluttered to the floor. This one was a one hundred dollar bill, crisp and brand new, tucked in there just for me. My mouth gaped open, but no words came out. None were necessary. The two notes told the story.

Of all the challenges I could put before you, homeschooling mother, as you begin this school year, the most valuable is to encourage you to begin each day with time in your heavenly Father's devotional book, the Bible. It contains words you can base your life on. It contains words of affirmation, challenge, instruction, comfort, and wisdom. Between the pages you will find God's love letter to you and more treasure than you could ever imagine. Don't let to-do lists, lesson plans, field trips, outside classes, extra curricular activities, or even family time keep you from beginning your homeschool day with time in your Father's book.

Application Question

What is most likely to distract you from spending time in God's Word--outside activities? Media? Sleep?

Action Step for This Week

Commit to spending time in God's Word first. As Chip Ingram, pastor and teacher of Living on the Edge Ministries says, "When you begin your day with the God of the Universe, no matter what else happens, it will be a pretty good day."

Prayer of Commitment

Lord, I confess I allow other things to take the place of my time with You. Sometimes I would rather stay in bed and sleep than have my quiet time. Other times I pack my day so full of activities there is not a minute left for You. You command us to seek first Your kingdom, and all the other parts will fall into place. Help me do that by giving You the first part of my day. I trust You to multiply the remaining time and help me glorify You.

SEPTEMBER

HOW DO YOU USE YOUR WORDS?

"The tongue has the power of life and death, and those who love it will eat its fruit."

Proverbs 18:21

Barnabas. His name, according to Acts 4:36, means "son of encouragement." To encourage means to "put courage into someone." I wonder how often we are a son (or daughter) of encouragement? How often do the words we speak into our children, our mates, and our friends lift them up rather than tear them down? Do we home in on the negative, while allowing the positive to go unnoticed? Do we fail to comment on tasks done well because "that's the way they should be done," while being quick to point out something undone? Do we deliver a compliment with a caveat, "You did a good job. I wish you would have done it sooner..."

Any reader of the book of James realizes that words are powerful. They are perhaps our most powerful instrument, both for good and for harm. Think back to your childhood. Was there one teacher who saw potential in you and spoke it aloud? For me it was a sixth-grade substitute English teacher. "You used colorful verbs," she said. "I enjoyed your paper. You will be a great writer someday." Twenty-five years later the words still resound. Twenty-five years later I am still reaching for that goal.

Take a moment today. Look carefully at your child. Look until you find something that is genuinely praiseworthy. Speak it aloud. Tell him how proud he makes you feel. Then point him to the future and give him a vision for what he can become if he continues in that good way. "I saw you help your sister when she fell off the swing. You were very compassionate to her. I'm proud of you. You will be a great daddy someday." Punctuate it with a hug and watch his eyes shine. "The tongue has the power of life and death, and those who love it will eat its fruit." (Proverbs 18:21)

Application Questions

1. How do you use your words?
2. Do you build people up or tear them down?

Action Step for This Week

Look carefully at each of your children until you find something genuinely praiseworthy. Speak words of praise aloud to them. Use your words to cast a vision for their future. Choose to speak words of edification to those within your circle of influence.

Prayer of Commitment

Lord, it is so easy to speak critical and damaging words instead of positive and uplifting ones. Please give me eyes to see the good in those around me and to verbalize words of praise to them. Help me use my words build up my family and not tear them down. Help the words of my mouth and the meditations of my heart be acceptable in Your sight, O Lord.

SEPTEMBER

THE DAY GOD SHOWED UP

"In the beginning, God created the heavens and the earth…"
Genesis 1:1

A biology lab met around my kitchen table one school year. It was a big step for me. Despite graduating from college with a degree in science, I somehow managed to dodge high school biology. The 100-item bug collection assignment in the first week of school convinced me that biology wasn't for me. By the time I reached college biology, we were way past bugs and into (literally) much safer subjects, like eyeballs and fetal pigs. When high school biology came around for my children, however, I was now the teacher, and avoidance was no longer an option.

Each of my co-op students arrived that first day. We set up the microscope and prepared to look at some pond water cultures. As we adjusted the fine magnification for an up-close look at our specimens, guess what happened? God showed up!

He wasn't pressed between the cover slip and the slide, nor was He swimming around in the slimy water with the paramecium. He certainly wasn't in the stench that filled our nostrils when we uncapped the samples after 5 days of incubating, but He was there!

Psalm 19:1 states that "the heavens declare the glory of God, and the skies proclaim the work of His hands." I'm not presuming to critique the Psalmist's work, but I think that verse could have just as accurately said, "the microscope declares the glory of God," because there in the tiny, normally unseen world captured on a 1"x2" slide was enough evidence of God's handiwork to silence the loudest critic. We saw means of respiration, locomotion, and reproduction, all packaged efficiently into an organism so small one thousand can fit into the dot of an "i." And these cells are the simplest of His creation!

The next time you take a moment during your homeschool day to look at, really look at, an aspect of God's creation with your children, beware! God just might show up.

Application Questions

1. What tone am I setting with my children as we study aspects of the physical world?

2. Do we slow down and talk about how all of creation displays evidence of our Creator, or do we merely satisfy the assignment and move on?

Action Step for This Week

The next time you study an aspect of the created world, guide your children to look for the qualities of God that each object displays. (Ex. Can you see in this specimen that God is artistic, detailed, precise, creative, orderly, etc.?)

Prayer of Commitment

Lord Jesus, your Word tells us You formed the earth and all that is in it. Forgive me for skipping right by the daily evidences of Your creativity all around me. Help me teach my children to see the many attributes of Yourself that You display in our world. Give us eyes to see and grateful hearts to appreciate all You have entrusted to us as stewards of this earth.

October

HOMESCHOOLING IS *HARD!*

OH, THE PLACES YOU WILL GO!

GRACE

YOU KNOW YOU'RE A HOMESCHOOLER WHEN...

HOMESCHOOLING IS *HARD!*

"Consider it pure joy, my brothers, whenever you face trials of many kinds, because you know that the testing of your faith develops perseverance. Perseverance must finish its work so that you may be mature and complete, not lacking anything.
James 1:2-4

How is your homeschooling going? During the past month, have you felt the urge to give up and send those ungrateful disobedient children back to school, and get on with your life?

I remember when it first dawned on me that homeschooling was hard. It came at the end of our first week of kindergarten. Despite daily phonics instruction, my five year old was still not reading!!

We may have begun kindergarten the week before, but it was the first day of class for me. The subject? Perseverance. You don't hear much about perseverance these days. We live in a world of instant grits, microwave popcorn, remote controls, and take-out chicken. It all points to instant results with little effort.

Homeschooling is not like that. Neither is parenting. Parenting is hard work. So is homeschooling. My grandmother used to say, "Anything worth having is worth working for." Now the phrase is, "No pain, no gain." Both remind me that godly, educated children don't just "happen." They are not the result of good curriculum, smart co-op teachers, or the finest SAT prep courses. Godly, educated children are the result of 18+ years of hard work, hours of prayer, countless sleepless nights, and lots of God's grace. They are the result of choosing to persevere, even when it's hard - especially when it's hard.

Application Questions
1. What aspect of homeschooling is discouraging to you right now?
2. Is homeschooling harder than you thought it would be?

Action Step for This Week

Read the Psalms of David and Hebrews 11and 12 for encouragement from the scriptures.

Prayer of Commitment

Lord, thank You for the examples of godly men and women who persevered despite incredible hardship. Thank You also for Your promise that we do not labor in vain. You see all the work we do in Your name, and You will reward me both in this life and in the life to come. Help me to keep my eyes on the finish line and run the race of life and homeschooling with patience and faith. (Hebrews 12:1)

OH, THE PLACES YOU WILL GO!

"Therefore I exhort first of all that supplications, prayers, intercessions, and giving of thanks be made for all men, for kings and all who are in authority, that we may lead a quiet and peaceable life in all godliness and reverence."

I Timothy 2:1-2

It was a surreal experience. On my right was United States Senator Lindsay Graham. On my left was United States Congressman Joe Wilson. Completing the trio was Senate hopeful Jim DeMint. And me. Me, who three months earlier thought that Wilson was a tennis ball company, grahams went with chocolate to make s'mores, and de mint was what you ate after de meal. Now I listened to their plans for our state and country and asked questions that were reasonably intelligent. To what did I owe this newfound political savvy? My 15-year-old politically interested home-schooled daughter.

Interested in the political process and wanting to earn her high school credit in Government, my daughter made contact with several of the local candidates running for political office and volunteered her services. The rest as they say, is history. Smart candidates recognize the goldmine of time, energy, and enthusiasm that belongs to most homeschoolers. They realize it doesn't take a rocket scientist to hand out stickers in a parade, staple yard signs together, prepare mailers, and waive signs at polling places. Each hour my daughter worked counted toward elusive Carnegie unit for Government. Each hour she worked taught her valuable things about the political process.

More than that though, our whole family has learned that our elected officials really do care about the people they serve. Each of the men took the time to thank my daughter for her service as warmly as if she had donated much more than time to their campaigns. They took time out of their busy schedules to tell stories of when they were 15 years old and working on their first campaigns. They recognized that the young people working with them are the future - citizens, voters, and possibly elected officials, and planted seeds of that vision in them.

If your family has never gotten involved in a political campaign, I urge you to consider it today. Choose a candidate whose views mirror yours and give their campaign headquarters a call. It is a great way to meet the men and women who represent us at the school board, county council, statehouse, and in Washington. Your children will be on their way to becoming an active part in our country's democracy, and you might even learn what House district you live in once and for all.

Application Questions

1. Have you and your family been passive or involved in the political process?
2. Have you ever considered volunteering to help a local candidate run for office?
3. Which candidates' or currently elected officials' platforms most closely align with a biblical worldview on current issues?
4. Is it important to you that your children learn the political process?

Action Step for This Week

Teach your children how to find a candidate or incumbent within your area whose political views most closely align with your own. Contact his/her office to volunteer.

Prayer of Commitment

Lord, it is so easy to be passive when it comes to government. There's a lot I don't understand, and sometimes it seems only the immoral and dishonest get elected. Please show me how You would like for our family to be a part of the political process. Help us to find a godly man or woman like Daniel or Mordecai to come alongside with our prayers, time, and effort.

GRACE

"In Him we have redemption through his blood, the forgiveness of sins, in accordance with the riches of God's grace that he lavished on us with all wisdom and understanding."

Ephesians 1:7-8

Grace is unmerited favor. The word appears 131 times in the Bible, with another 49 or so forms of the word. Most of us understand it in the theological sense, but do we understand it in or daily lives? Better yet, do we practice it?

What does grace look like? Who does grace look like? This is what grace looks like to me. Grace sees the things I have done, not the things I haven't. Grace sees how far I have come instead of how far I still have to go. Grace sees my intent, not my end result. Grace sees how much I deserve and gives me so much more. Grace sees the punishment I deserve and gives forgiveness instead.

Grace says, "I understand; I forgive you," instead of pointing out my shortcomings. Grace cries with me when I fail. Grace gives second, third, and fourth chances. Grace assumes the best. Grace says, "Welcome," instead of "You don't belong here." Grace says, "Try again," instead of "Why bother?" Grace notices our differences and rejoices.

Grace recognizes that my children are still under construction. Grace trusts that the Holy Spirit can lead my family in a different direction than someone else's, but both are from the Lord. Grace thinks before she speaks, and sometimes chooses not to speak at all. Grace asks instead of assumes. Grace remembers that "God so loved the world." Grace serves unselfishly, with pure motives. Best of all, grace smiles.

Dear homeschooling mother, breathe grace!

Application Questions

1. Do you have more of a tendency to exhibit grace or criticism?
2. Do you bestow grace on others, yet have a hard time bestowing it on yourself?

Action Step for This Week

When you feel like you've failed, graciously give yourself another chance.

Prayer of Commitment

Lord Jesus, sometimes I am so critical. Help me look for the best in other people and in myself. Help me realize that we are all at different stages in our spiritual growth, and that You are at work in all of us. Help me believe that 'He who began a good work in (me) will be faithful to complete it.' (Philippians 1:6) Lord, help me today, if I must err, to err on the side of grace.

YOU KNOW YOU'RE A HOMESCHOOLER WHEN...

"Laughter does the heart good, like a medicine."
Proverbs 17:22

Have you noticed that the homeschooling community has a culture all its own? For those of you who are new to the world of homeschooling, let me clue you in on a few telltale signs that a family is homeschooling.

You know you're homeschooling when...
- You no longer take family vacations; you take "field trips" instead.
- Your child asks for *The Journals of Lewis and Clark* for her 13th birthday.
- Your husband knows he must ask permission before consuming anything in the refrigerator, because it might be a science experiment.
- Your children spell "surely" with an "h" because that's how Shurley Grammar is spelled.
- You rejoice when a spider lays an egg case on your window screen, because you are studying arachnids this month.
- You donate blood and bring your children along because the Red Cross doesn't do field trips.
- If you see a mom with children out during school hours, you assume she is a homeschooler, instead of truant, especially if she's wearing denim.
- Your library book box has wheels.
- The cost of your monthly library fines exceeds your water bill.
- You sing the books of the Bible song as you wash dishes.

Application Question
Do you have a tendency to take homeschooling too seriously and forget to laugh?

Action Step for This Week

Read the above list to your family at the dinner table and try to come up with a few "You Know You're a Homeschooler When..." statements of your own. Laugh together.

Prayer of Commitment

Lord, I know that You laugh, because we are created in Your image with the capacity to laugh. Help me not take homeschooling so seriously that I forget to have fun. Give me some fun ideas for ways to introduce more laughter into our homeschool this week.

November

JESUS' TIME-MANAGEMENT TOOL

GIVING THANKS WHEN YOU DON'T FEEL THANKFUL

DON'T STRUGGLE ALONE

BECAUSE KIDS MATTER TO GOD

JESUS' TIME-MANAGEMENT TOOL

"Early in the morning, I lay my requests before you and wait in expectation."

Psalm 5:3

I tried daytimers and planners, schedules and how-to books. I tried getting up earlier and staying up later. I studied efficiency and prioritizing, all to no avail. There were never enough hours in my day, and I never accomplished all I hoped to do. Finally I discovered what I feel is the best time management tool we can ever employ- our daily quiet time.

Several years ago I began the consistent practice of starting my day with an appointment with God. The Bible tells us that Jesus did this. "Very early in the morning, while it was yet dark, Jesus went away to a solitary place to pray." (Mark 1:35) My quiet time contains many of the same elements you have in yours, I'm sure. I spend time reading a portion of the Bible, praying for the needs of my family and others, and praising and thanking God for who He is and what He is doing in my life.

After I have walked through those components, I begin my "strategizing" for the day. First, I think through the day ahead. Sometimes I sketch it out on a piece of paper. I draw up a tentative schedule, or maybe just a "to do" list of the things I hope to accomplish. Next, I pray. During my prayer, I give the Lord "my" day. I ask Him to take away those things that are not a part of His plan for me. I ask Him to maximize my energy and resources so I can be most effective. I ask Him to help me see people as He sees them and to conduct myself accordingly. I ask Him to bring to my consciousness what I most need to do, to be, and to say that day.

Then I stop talking and let Him talk. Sometimes, during those times when I am quiet and listening for His voice, a person or a need will come to mind. I add them to my list. Sometimes a great idea will come to me. I know those are from the Lord! Occasionally, I rethink something on my list and take it off, or I might replace it with a better idea or approach.

It is during this time of quietly listening that I submit my will to the Lord's and get my marching orders from the King. The results of Jesus' quiet times were that he always did those things that pleased the Father. (John 8:28) This is my goal too. I encourage you to give Jesus' time management tip a try. The results will amaze you!

Application Questions
1. Are you frustrated and overwhelmed by your 'to do" list?
2. Are you busy but not productive?
3. Do you feel as though you don't have time to pray and read your Bible?

Action Step for This Week
Commit to meet daily with God in prayer and Bible reading. At the end of the week, evaluate the results.

Prayer of Commitment
Lord, Jesus was our example of how we should live our lives on this earth. If Jesus, Who was God in the flesh, thought it was important to meet with You each day, then I know I should. I commit to devote time every day this week in Bible reading and prayer. As I submit each day to You, help me listen to Your voice and obey what You tell me to do and not to do. Help me be efficient and effective in the tasks You give me. Bless the work of my hands as I submit it to You.

GIVING THANKS WHEN YOU DON'T FEEL THANKFUL

" I n everything give thanks, for this is the will of God for you."
1 Thessalonians 5:18

If you've been a Christian for any length of time, you have already realized this spiritual principle: battles are won or lost in our minds. Not in some new-agey way, or mind-over-matter-and -deny-the-reality way, or even in a "power of positive thinking" way, but in a biblical way.

I experienced this truth during a time when our family was hit with a series of illnesses. I discovered it was easy to maintain my focus when one person got sick, or even when one person at a time got sick, or even when everyone but the mommy got sick, but when all of the above happened, it hit really hard.

One morning during my quiet time with the Lord, I read 1 Thessalonians 5:18, "In everything give thanks, for this is the will of God for you." I realized this is where the victory is won—in the choices we make. Being thankful is a choice, not a feeling. I can choose to feel sorry for myself because I am cooped up in a house that sounds like a Tuberculosis ward during an epidemic, or I can be thankful for family and friends who brought by meals and groceries because I couldn't get out.

I can whine about having to set the alarm clock to give a feverish child a dose of medicine, or I can be thankful for her sweet, softly whispered, "I love you, Mommy. You're the best nurse ever." I can complain about having no energy, or I can be thankful for those times of inactivity when all of us cuddle together on a couch to read a book because that is the only thing we feel like doing. I can complain about how long we've been sick, or I can be thankful that we will, unlike many, be well again. I cannot control my circumstances, but I can control how I react to them.

Speaker, writer, and pastor Chuck Swindoll is often quoted as saying, "The longer I live, the more I realize the impact of attitude on life. Attitude, to me, is more important than facts. It is more important than the past, than education, than money, than circumstances, than failure, than successes, than what other people think or say or do.

"It is more important than appearance, giftedness or skill. It will make or break a company... a church... a home. The remarkable thing is we have a choice everyday regarding the attitude we will embrace for that day. We cannot change our past... we cannot change the fact that people will act in a certain way. We cannot change the inevitable. The only thing we can do is play on the one string we have, and that is our attitude. I am convinced that life is 10% what happens to me and 90% of how I react to it. And so it is with you... we are in charge of our attitudes."

May we be victorious through the attitude we choose to embrace. In everything give thanks!

Application Questions
1. What is the most difficult aspect of your life right now?
2. Are you willing to give thanks to God for it, trusting that He will use it for your good?

Action Step for This Week
Post the above quote from Chuck Swindoll and 1 Thessalonians 5:18 in a prominent place in your home. Commit to glorify God through your attitude this week.

Prayer of Commitment
Lord, I confess that sometimes my attitude is not thankful or positive. Sometimes I don't really believe You are at work in the difficult circumstances in my life. Sometimes I forget You didn't come to make us comfortable; You came to make us holy. Help me, this week, to set the example before my children of what it means to give thanks in everything.

DON'T STRUGGLE ALONE

"It is not good that man should be alone."
Genesis 2:8

"I don't want to bother you."
"I knew the conversation would be depressing, and I didn't want to bring you down."
"I hate to admit that I am struggling."
"I don't want you to think less of me."

I have heard these words in the past week as dear friends have called with cries for help. What disturbs me most are not the phone calls, but the length of time friends have been suffering in silence, alone.

We've all heard the cliché "Go to the throne, and not to the phone." It reminds us that we should go to God first when we encounter difficulties. Somehow, I think this advice has caused us to feel like going to God should always be enough. Stay with me, I am not about to commit heresy! I agree that ultimately God is our Sustainer, Provider, Rescuer, Wisdom-giver, Earth-mover, and on and on. We find our sufficiency in Him.

However, even though Adam had a perfect sinless relationship with God in the garden, enjoying fellowship, conversation, and communion, at the end of the day God said, "It is not good that man should be alone." (Genesis 2:8) We know Adam wasn't technically alone, because He had God, but he was alone in that he had no other human being with which to share his life. He had no one "like him" to share his laughter, his frustrations, his anger, his wonder, and yes, his struggles.

As believers, we are called to "bear one another's burdens, and so fulfill the law of Christ." (Galatians 6:12) When a person enters into a relationship with Christ, the first thing God does is put each believer into a family -- the family of God. He does this because we need each other. Ecclesiastes 4: 9-10, 12 says, "Two are better than one, because they have a good reward for labor. For if they fall, one will lift up his companion. But woe to him who is alone when he falls, for he has no one to help him up. Though one may be overpowered by another, two can withstand him. . . And a threefold cord is not quickly broken."

Homeschooling mothers, if you are struggling, please do not struggle alone! Don't be the little fluffy sheep the wolf lures away from the herd so he can devour. Go to the throne first. In many situations, this may be all you need to do. Always begin there. Then, if you are still struggling, go to your husband or a trusted, godly friend. Go to your Sunday school class or your fellow homeschoolers. This is why homeschoolers all over the country have monthly support group meetings -- so no one has to struggle alone.

Application Questions
1. Do you have a tendency to suffer alone? Why?
2. Have you developed enough of a support network that you have at least a few trusted friends whom you can call when you are struggling?
3. How can you be more aware of others around you who might be struggling?

Action Step for This Week
If you do not have a support network, either through your homeschool group, church family, or physical family, take steps to begin to develop this. Remember, "To have a friend, one must show himself friendly." (Proverbs 18:24)

Prayer of Commitment
Lord, sometimes I try to be a Lone Ranger. It's hard to admit to someone else that I need help, or things aren't going well, because I think it's not very spiritual. Surely my relationship with You should be enough, right? But I know You have placed believers in families since the beginning of time. Help me to be willing to be vulnerable and share my struggles with those I trust. If there is no one in my life I feel like I can trust right now, please send a friend my way. Help me reach out to others, and in so doing, make friends I might otherwise not have had. Thank You for being my best Friend.

BECAUSE KIDS MATTER GOD

" B y wisdom a house is built, and though understanding it is established; through knowledge its rooms are filled with rare and beautiful treasures."
Proverbs 24:3-4

Our church recently began the AWANA program. Emblazoned on all its leaders' shirts are the words "AWANA- Because Kids Matter to God." Often as parents we tend to think of our children's worth in terms of who they will become when they are grown. We must remember our children are valuable to God (and to us) just as they are--sticky faces, endless questions, perpetual wiggle, selective hearing, and all.

We hear God's heart in the Gospel of Matthew when he rebuked his disciples for treating a child as insignificant, "Suffer the little children to come unto me, and do not forbid them, for of such is the kingdom of God." (Matthew 19:14) When they were squabbling over who was the most important in the kingdom, "He called a little child and had him stand among them. He said, '...unless you change and become like little children, you will never enter the kingdom of heaven...and whoever welcomes a child like this in my name welcomes me.'"

When you get frustrated with your children's immaturity and helplessness and wonder if they will ever grow up, take heart. It is this same childish nature that gives the sweetest bedtime hugs, always forgives when we're unkind, and teaches us more about God and ourselves than any adult Bible study leader.

Homeschooling mother, you are doing a great job! You have chosen to give this portion of your life to educate some of God's little ones. I think part of the "Well done!" we will hear will be because of the years we have given to raising our children in the nurture and admonition of the Lord. Homeschooling - Because Kids Matter to God!

Application Questions
  1. What areas of immaturity frustrate you about your children?
  2. Are they areas of foolishness (sin that needs to be corrected), or childishness (immaturity that will be corrected by time and growth)?

Action Step for This Week

After you have evaluated the areas of frustration, determine an appropriate course of action to help your children grow. Thank God for the sweet aspects of childhood.

Prayer of Commitment

Lord, sometimes I get so frustrated with my children's immaturity. Help me have a proper perspective on what areas of their lives need correction and which areas need training. Give me the wisdom to determine what is sin and what is childishness. Give me the patience to consistently train them to honor you in all they do. Remind me to take time to relish the sweet, special, unique joys of having young children in my life. Thank You for the precious gift of my children.

December

SNEEZES, SNAKES, AND LIFE'S BIG QUESTIONS

UNSOCIALIZED?

JESUS WAS A TEACHER, TOO

WHAT HAPPENS WHEN WE OBEY

SNEEZES, SNAKES, AND LIFE'S BIG QUESTIONS

"If any of you lack wisdom, let him ask of God who gives to all men liberally without finding fault, and it will be given to him."
James 1:5

I recently did something I haven't done in a very long time. I went to the zoo with my seventeen-year-old daughter and twin four-year olds. She was babysitting; I was along as another pair or hands. Our primary mission was to try to catch a glimpse of the elusive baby koala, Owen. The process was not an easy one. I had forgotten how complicated a simple outing could be with small children. Car seat (x2). Lunch (x2). Backpacks (x2). Raincoats, band aides (just in case), and dollars for the carousel. When did the price change from quarters to dollars? Obviously sometime in the last fourteen years or so.

I had also forgotten how much fun it was to interact with four-year-olds who tell you everything. "My daddy works out, that's why he has 100 muscles," and "My hair is short because my sister was playing with the scissors, and I got in the way."

I had forgotten, too, that little legs tire easily, and piggyback rides are the easiest way to transport small children who ask, "Let me hold you!" I had forgotten how sweet it felt to hold a little hand in mine, and how wide a smile could get when riding a "flying tiger" on the carousel.

Hundreds of questions kept me thinking. "Why is that snake sticking his tongue out at me?" "Can fish hold their breath?" "Do alligators get tired of eating fish all the time?" I felt like a Jeopardy contestant working her way to the jackpot after I fielded category after category of potential brain stumpers.

I had forgotten how good it felt to answer black and white questions that have only one answer. The questions are harder now that I have young adults. I can't fake any of the answers, because the stakes are higher than any Jeopardy game.

Homeschooling mom, if you have young children, savor every moment. Even when they sneeze on you. Hug them before they get too cool for such nonsense. And encourage them to ask questions. Someday those simple questions will pave the way for harder ones.

If you are the parent of older children or young adults, savor every moment. Even if they bring you to your knees in prayer. Especially if they bring you to your feet in praise. And don't fear the questions. Claim the promise of James 1:5: "If any of you lack wisdom, let him ask of God who gives to all men liberally without finding fault, and it will be given to him."

God bless you as you parent your children in faith!

Application Questions

1. What aspects of life with small children tend to make you most weary?
2. Which are the most fun?
3. What questions have your children (younger or older) asked you lately that made you really stop and think?

Action Step for This Week

Commit to listen -- really listen the next time your children ask questions. Ask a few of your own and see what type of conversation develops.

Prayer of Commitment

Lord, in Daniel nine, Daniel talks about how You inclined your ear to hear his prayer. Help me, Lord, to listen like You do. Help me be quick to hear and slow to speak, so my children will find in me a sympathetic and interested listener. As I take the time to listen, help them to open up their hearts and minds to me, especially my older children. Give me wisdom to know how to answer their questions with godly, insightful wisdom that can only come from spending time with You. Thank you, Lord that You always take time to listen to me.

JOY IN THE JOURNEY

UNSOCIALIZED?

"To have a friend, one must show himself friendly."
Proverbs 18:24

We've all heard them – the ever-present, always-expected questions about how homeschooled children learn to socialize. We can all parrot back the answers, "Why, they learn to interact with other people by learning to get along with their siblings, not to mention all the adults they get to talk to as we go about our unconventional school day."

Our homeschooled children have many opportunities to learn virtues such as patience and kindness, gentleness and self-control as they go through their days in our homeschools. And yes, most of them can carry on marvelous, articulate conversations with adults, especially those who enjoy interacting with them. There is, however, a gap in their social experience.

I have had the opportunity over 17 years to watch how our homeschooled children handle social situations. For the most part, I like what I see. The students are respectful to the adults who are in charge. They conduct themselves appropriately for the situation. They participate with enthusiasm.

One thing is noteworthy, however. Almost across the board, our students do not go out of their comfort zones to interact with students they do not know. I am sure this is not unique to homeschooled students. In one recent situation, I observed several students who knew each other. They clustered together chattering enthusiastically. There were also several newcomers to the group. They stood to the side without interacting.

In another situation, a brave soul approached the newcomers and spoke to one of the young ladies. She attempted to start a conversation with the newcomer, but after a few monosyllabic answers in return, she gave up the attempt and went back to the comfortable group.

What are the lessons to be learned here? Are homeschooled students (perish the thought!) unsocialized?! I think not. I do think, however, there are some social lessons they can learn that all children need, regardless of where they go to school.

The first lesson is this: Human nature gravitates toward what is comfortable. This is why people of all ages approach a group to see who they know so they can join them. If you're not convinced, watch yourself at a church gathering or homeschool support group meeting. You probably do a good job of welcoming newcomers, but if you're honest, you must admit you prefer to interact with those who are most familiar to you. Put yourself in a newcomer's place and imagine how it would feel to approach a group in which you knew no one. This is a good way to encourage our children and ourselves to be more aware of newcomers. We need to encourage our children through our words and our example to purposefully seek those who are new and welcome them in. How precious just one friendly face can be!

Lesson number two is this: "To have a friend, one must show himself friendly." (Proverbs 18: 24) We must train our children how to respond to an attempt at friendship. You can role play and practice the fine art of conversation. "Hi, my name is Lori. What is your name?" "My name is John. Have you ever played on a basketball league before?" "No, I haven't, but I play in my neighborhood all the time." This type of give and take is much more conducive to a potential friendship than monosyllabic answers that discourage a tentative attempt to reach out.

Lesson number three is a good one with which to conclude. Just like we don't expect our children to know how to add and subtract without instruction, we also can't expect them to know how to relate to their peers in social situations without instruction. Preparing them in advance of a social situation can set them up for success. "Today's the first Park Day. There will be some new friends there we haven't met yet. Let's be sure to look out for them. I can't wait to see what new friends the Lord is going to send our way today."

Seventeen years ago I attended my first homeschool support group meeting. I don't remember who welcomed me that day, but I know I was welcomed. I came home feeling wanted and cared for. What a precious gift! Let's teach our children how to practice the fine art of giving friendship away. Friendship is one of the few things in this life we can give away generously and come away richer for having done it.

Application Questions

1. In social situations, do you tend to gravitate toward those you know or are you willing to reach out to those you don't?
2. How about your children?
3. Talk with your children about situations where they have been the newcomer and ask them how it felt when someone did or didn't reach out to them.
4. What can you do to practice reaching out to new people?

Action Steps for This Week

Role play with your children how to introduce themselves to other children and adults. Practice a few conversational openers, and then intentionally target a few new people to interact with. Report back on the results over dinner time that night.

Prayer of Commitment

Lord, all of us feel a little awkward approaching someone we don't know. I know You command us to practice hospitality, and part of that command is helping a new person feel welcome wherever we are. Help my children and me to be more intentional about reaching out to new people. I believe You are going to bless our efforts by sending some very special friends our way as a result of stepping outside our comfort zones. Thank You for the people over the years who have made a special effort to extend friendship to us.

DECEMBER

JESUS WAS A TEACHER, TOO

"And He taught them many things by parables,"
Mark 4:2

Have you ever thought about the fact that you and Jesus have the same profession? No, not carpentry, teaching! Jesus was a Master Teacher. Even though you spend many hours teaching subjects like spelling and math, I know the heartbeat of why you homeschool your children is so you can impart spiritual truths that will impact their lives, and our world, forever. This was Jesus' goal too. As you and I seek to become master teachers of our children, we can learn from the Master Teacher, Jesus Christ.

One of the most effective ways Jesus imparted spiritual truth was through the use of storytelling. Parables formed the basis of many of His lessons to His disciples. His parables still impact us today. Who doesn't feel the lostness of the prodigal son, the pain of his father, or the jealousy of his older brother?

Remember the story of the foolish man who built his house upon the sand? When the rains came down and the floods came up, did you feel the waves as the house on the sand went *splat*?

Even God the Father used a parable when He spoke through Nathan the prophet to King David after his encounter with Bathsheba. Nathan told a parable to engage King David's mind, arouse the appropriate emotions, and engage his heart. Then he pointed his finger and said, "Thou art the man!" Thus remains a powerful lesson over 3,000 years later.

You can use this same technique when you interact with your children. Whether your purpose is to spur them on to love and good works, confront and convict them of sin, or praise and encourage their good behavior, a story or word picture can take ordinary words and make them powerful and memorable. Take a lesson from the Master Teacher. Pray and ask Him for just the right story, and watch how God will communicate His truths through you!

Application Question

Are there areas in your children's lives that might be best addressed through the use of a parable?

Action Step for This Week

Pray and ask God for the right story at the right time to communicate the message He would have you share with your children. Ask Him to apply the message to their hearts for His purpose.

Prayer of Commitment

Lord Jesus, you are the Master Teacher. Help me learn from You how best to communicate Your truths to my children. If there is an area where they need to be challenged, a sin about which I should confront them, or a situation in which they need encouragement, please help me recognize it. Give me insight and wisdom to know just what words to share and what story to tell to accomplish Your purpose in their hearts and lives. Help me be sensitive to your timing, and trust You for the results.

WHAT HAPPENS WHEN WE OBEY

"In this world, you will have tribulation, but be of good cheer, I have overcome the world."

John 16:33

During a conversation with a friend, we discussed the fact that as Christians, we often think when we are obedient to Christ, things should go easier for us. After all, shouldn't God reward us for being obedient? Let's take this line of reasoning a step further and apply it to homeschooling. When we make the choice to homeschool our children, especially when it is for spiritual reasons, shouldn't things be easy?

When we give out their daily assignments, shouldn't our children smile angelically as they say, "Yes, ma'am, I'll get right to it?" Every so often, shouldn't they thank us sincerely for the sacrifices we've made in order to homeschool them? Shouldn't their eyes light up with eagerness as we share the day's Bible lesson while they ask insightful and spiritually discerning questions? Shouldn't they play nicely and share with their siblings every day because of the precious bond they are developing with each other because of being homeschooled? And shouldn't our husbands volunteer to teach Bible, higher math and science, as well as do all the household repairs in a timely manner while working 70 hours a week to earn a living sufficient to support our family?

Unfortunately, the reality of life on this earth is that sometimes being obedient to God's will for our lives makes our lives harder, not easier. Jesus said in John 16:33, "In this world, you will have tribulation, but be of good cheer, I have overcome the world." But friends, let us lift our eyes and take the long view of our homeschooling journey in light of eternity. Let us "press on toward the goal to win the prize of which God has called me heavenward in Christ Jesus." "Let us not grow weary in doing good, for we will reap a harvest if we do not faint!" (Galatians 6:9)

Application Questions

1. When you get disappointed or discouraged, is it because you expect God to reward your obedience with an easy life?
2. Is this expectation biblical?

Action Step for This Week

Read 2 Corinthians 1:1-12 to get Paul's perspective on obedience and suffering.

Prayer of Commitment

Dear Lord, thank You for the privilege of serving You by serving my family through homeschooling. Help me be willing to serve You whether or not I see the benefits of my obedience during my lifetime. Keep me mindful of Your example, how You took upon Yourself the form of a servant, humbling Yourself in obedience to the Father, and submitting to death on the cross to serve me. (Philippians 2:5-8) Help me remember Your promise not to forget my work and labor of love done in Your name toward Your children. (Hebrews 6:10)

January

NEW YEAR'S INTROSPECTION

TEACHING THEM TO GO

WHEN PLANS MEET REALITY

HOMESCHOOLERS ARE *RICH!*

NEW YEAR'S INTROSPECTION

"This is my prayer, that your love may abound more and more in knowledge and depth of insight, so that you may be able to discern what is best and may be pure and blameless until the day of Christ, filled with the fruit of righteousness that comes through Jesus Christ - to the glory and praise of God!"
Philippians 1:9-11

It was a New Year's Day I have never forgotten. New years tend to make me introspective, but on this day I was especially thoughtful. As I pondered my character flaws, I was overwhelmed with discouragement. Most obvious to me that day was a lack of gentleness in my life and heart. Quick tempered, sharp, sometimes even downright unkind, I definitely didn't fit the pattern of scripture for a godly wife and mother.

Thankfully, before I had wallowed too long in the "slough of despond," the Holy Spirit reminded me that in Christ, there is "no condemnation," (Romans 8), and any condemning words were coming from the enemy, the "father of lies," not the Lord. God encouraged me with these words, "being confident of this, that He who began a good work in you will carry it on to completion." (Philippians 1:6) It was good for me to recognize the areas of my character that needed improvement, but I needed more than sorrow to begin the process of change.

First, I confessed my shortcomings (sin) to the Lord. Next I asked Him to give me the power every day to begin to change. Lastly, I asked two special friends to pray for me daily and keep me accountable.

So often at mid-year, we look back and see everything we haven't accomplished, the ways we have failed, and the person we are that falls so far short of the person we want to be.

I encourage you to make an honest assessment of yourself. You might even want to bring your spouse in on the appraisal – ouch! Then find scripture verses that apply to your area of need and commit those areas of your life to the Lord's control. Finally, find an accountability partner.

Rather than empty regrets that bring nothing but discouragement, a godly plan of action can begin the process of transformation in your life. As you begin homeschooling this year to the glory of God, "this is my prayer, that your love may abound more and more in knowledge and depth of insight, so that you may be able to discern what is best and may be pure and blameless until the day of Christ, filled with the fruit of righteousness that comes through Jesus Christ - to the Glory and praise of God!" (Philippians 1:9-11)

Application Question

What areas of your character fail to measure up to the fruit of the Spirit in Galatians 5:22-23?

Action Step for This Week

Choose one aspect of your character that needs improvement and commit to follow the action steps listed above. Watch how God enables you to grow in this area as you submit it to Him.

Prayer of Commitment

Lord, I know I need Your help to be a godly mother and wife. Sometimes the fruit of the Spirit is not evident in my life. More than anything else, I want my life to glorify You. I confess I am struggling with _____. Help me to submit _____ (my tongue, my temper, my stewardship etc.) to You so you can change me. Thank You I have the promise of Philippians 1:6 that tells me that (You) who began a good work in me will carry it on to completion.

TEACHING THEM TO GO

"Go therefore and make disciples of every nation..."
Matthew 28:19

It happens every year about January. The realization strikes that more than half the school year is over and you are nowhere near accomplishing everything you hoped to this school year. Our family had this experience recently. It was January. Not by the calendar, but in terms of my oldest daughter's homeschool education. She was a junior and it was time for the SAT, college visits, and typing up the transcript. We had been very careful to plot out the courses she needed to take to make her high school education complete. We were not as organized in plotting out the "life experiences" she needed before she graduated from Hatcher's Christian Academy. But thankfully it was January, and not May, and there was still time to fill in the blanks.

One of the goals for our children was for them to have a significant cross-cultural mission experience while they were still living in our home. Our primary goal in homeschooling has been to raise and educate the next generation of soldiers in the army of Christ. One of the most important jobs for Christians is to fulfill our Lord's last charge to his disciples, "Go therefore and make disciples of every nation…" (Matthew 28:19) We train them in English, math, science, and social studies, but how much time do we spend training them to win others to Christ?

To help accomplish this goal, we planned a family mission trip to Mexico. We and another homeschooling family worked with missionaries who have spent the last 15 years planting churches in Baja California, Mexico. Our goal was for our children to minister and serve alongside us as we reached out to the Mexican men, women, and children.

In preparation, our "curriculum" included teaching our children to share their testimonies, present the gospel, and give a brief devotional from the Bible. We practiced on each other and during outreach at our church. Leading up to the trip, we were in weekly communication with our missionary hosts learning everything we could about Mexico, the town they lived in, and the people they are giving their lives to reach.

As we plot our children's education, it is so easy to get lost in the academics and neglect the spiritual opportunities that will shape and prepare them for service to the Lord. I challenge you to look at the big picture - why you're doing what you're doing, and what will make your homeschooling experience a success by the standards that really matter (Hint: it has nothing to do with the SAT scores). Then pray. Ask God for an opportunity to introduce your children to the wonderful world of missions, both here and abroad. You never know what God has in mind for your children... or for you!

Application Questions

1. What opportunities have your children had to learn about and experience missions?
2. Do you have a plan for training them to share their faith?
3. Is there a mission group or short-term mission opportunity you could explore as a family?

Action Step for the Week

Pray and ask God to show you how you can explore missions as a family.

Prayer of Commitment

Lord, what a marvelous opportunity we have in homeschooling to train our children to have Your heart for the world. I know Your goal is to use the church to reach the world; what a privilege to be a part of that grand plan! Help us to know how best to expose our family to a cross-cultural mission experience in Your way and in Your timing. Help us to be willing to go where You tell us to go, knowing that in Your presence is fullness of joy.

WHEN PLANS MEET REALITY

"B ut seek first the kingdom of God and His righteousness, and all these things will be added unto you."
Matthew 6:33

By now the holiday season is over. Hopefully, amidst the activity of the season you also took time to rest, make some precious memories with your family, and catch up on things you neglected during the first half of the school year. Soon you will sit down to write those mid-year reports, tie up the loose ends of the first semester, and begin to plan for the second half of the school year.

It is often very discouraging and disheartening to hold the first semester's accomplishments up against the plumb line of planning. Somehow that history text has grown in volume, and you have fallen quite short of the half-way point where you had hoped to be. That month when Jr. got bogged down on multiplication tables, and you had to stop going forward in the text and break out the remedial practice pages put a serious delay on your plan for finishing the book this year. And then there was the two weeks when everyone came down with a stomach virus. Of course, everyone didn't come down with it all at once, but one person got sick every three days, so the "crud" lasted forever and the Health Department considered hanging a "Quarantined" sign on the door. Each separate delay didn't seem like a big deal, but somehow your homeschooling has fallen short of where you had hoped to be, and you are quite discouraged.

Take heart, homeschooling mom. Just as Christmas is about the fact that God gave fallen man a second chance at redemption, so second semesters are our second chance to redeem our homeschooling year. Our God is a God of second chances!

How does one begin again? First you must adjust your expectations. We all set high and lofty goals for our school years, only to realize later they were a bit unrealistic. If Jr. needed extra help in math. and you are behind in the textbook, then you are exactly where you need to be. Remember your goal is mastery not completion. A fully completed math text and a child who cannot do his multiplication tables is not success. There is no rule that says you can't carry your text over into the next school year if need be. That is the beauty of homeschooling – you can adjust your plan to meet your child's needs.

In some cases, like that of the multiplying history book, completion will simply require adding extra pages to your reading schedule, buckling down, and getting it done. Watch your children though. If their eyes begin to glaze over after the first 20 pages, and you plow on anyway, what are you really accomplishing? Once again, your goal is mastery. It is better to cover less material and really learn it.

Lastly, there will be time, like the virulent virus weeks, you simply cannot redeem. It is these times, like the days you stopped school to help a neighbor in need, or the week you took off to nurse Grandma back to health, that the Lord redeems for you.

Oh, your children won't miraculously know calculus when they didn't before, but God will multiply the learning that does take place and even "fill in the gaps" in ways you can't explain. He will provide help in an area that allows you to gain ground. He will provide learning opportunities that you could have never engineered yourself.

Best of all He will be your family's teacher. Sometimes academically, but also in those life lessons that teach us that sometimes schedules and plans need to be set aside to minister in His name. He restores what was "lost," and brings benefits of which you never dreamed. So work hard this semester. Be a diligent, faithful steward of the precious privilege of homeschooling, but also trust God for those things you cannot do.

Application Questions

1. What are the areas in which your children have fallen behind in their school work?
2. Were your goals too lofty or was it simply a matter of a lack of diligence?
3. Were these goals delayed by circumstances beyond your control?

Action Step for This Week

Evaluate each area and develop a plan to persevere, catch up, or set aside.

Prayer of Commitment

Lord, we are half-way through the school year, and we are behind in some areas. If we are behind because of a lack of diligence or discipline on my part, I confess this to You and ask You to help me do better in the second semester. If we are behind because of circumstances beyond our control, I ask You to show me which areas need to be made up, which we should continue on as we are going, and which should be set aside for a while. Thank You for the promise in James 1:5 that says if I lack wisdom, I can ask You for it and You will give it to me in abundance. I commit the second half of my school year to You.

HOMESCHOOLERS ARE *RICH!*

"The blessings of the Lord make one rich!"
Proverbs 10:22

I have the opportunity to talk to many people about the subject of home-schooling. They all ask the same question eventually, "Why do you homeschool?" Sometimes I answer, "For a quality education." Other times I say, "Because it's an efficient and effective way to teach several children at one time." Other times I say, "It gives us an opportunity to maximize our children's strengths and work on their weaknesses." My favorite answer though, is, "It's a wonderful, rich lifestyle." Have you ever thought about how rich you are if you are able to homeschool your children?

Looking back over 17+ years of homeschooling, I can't begin to recount all the awesome, exciting, one-of-a-kind experiences we've had simply because we have chosen to educate our children at home. The trip to Washington, DC, and the special VIP tour of the White House; the chance to fly in a Cessna over Columbia; the hundreds of "play dates" with friends during "school hours;" the poetry recitals in the garden of the Governor's Mansion; the chance to lobby for legislation that will impact our family; the tour of a gold mine; the chance to watch baby Loggerhead turtles be excavated from a nest and released to the sea; the hours and hours spent reading great books to my children; the Feast of Purim play and Passover Seder; camping trips; tours of courtrooms, jail cells, nature centers, historical sites, rock quarries, doughnut shops, forests and farms; teaching my children to read and to memorize Scripture; learning to "crab" from a dock on Hunting Island; petting a snake, a possum, a llama, a camel, and a Red-tailed hawk; walks on the beach, the mountains, the cities, and little towns are all experiences we might not have had if we weren't homeschooling.

I could go on and on. Remember, these experiences span almost two decades! In between every one of these "mountain top" experiences of homeschooling were many days of multiplication tables, spelling lessons, and just plain hard work. The majority of our time was spent "doing school" in the traditional way, but oh, the joy we experienced when one of those incredible learning adventures just "happened."

Could we have had these experiences if we hadn't homeschooled? Maybe, but I don't think so. I think we would have been so caught up in the traditional system of "doing school" that we wouldn't have been free to do school as only homeschoolers can.

If you've had your noses buried in books this winter, it's time to take them out, put your "adventure boots" on, and go make a memory. Remember, we homeschoolers are RICH, so let's live like we are!!!

Application Question

What are some of the best memories you have of special field trips or adventures you might not have experienced if you hadn't chosen to homeschool?

Action Step for This Week

Ask your children around the dinner table about their favorite home-schooling memories. Determine to plan at least one field trip a month between now and the end of the school year. Remember you are not just scheduling a learning experience, you are making a memory.

Prayer of Commitment

Lord, sometimes I get so bogged down in textbooks and workbooks, lesson plans and homework I forget the best learning takes place outside the classroom. Help me plan several fun field trips before the end of the school year. Remind me there is much more to learn than facts and figures, and help me thoroughly enjoy our field trips without feeling guilty about the "school" we are leaving behind. Help us also make great family memories as we experience your world together."

February

DUST BALLS, STANDARDIZED TESTING, AND GRACE

DON'T DESPISE THE DAY OF SMALL THINGS

DO FEW THINGS, AND DO THEM WELL

THE PRIVILEGE OF TRAINING A CHILD

DUST BALLS, STANDARDIZED TESTING, AND GRACE

"This one thing I do, forgetting what is behind and straining toward what is ahead, I press on toward the goal to win the prize for which God has called me heavenward."
Philippians 3:13-14

Have you ever noticed how the bright spring sunshine streaming in the window brings to light all the dust balls, fur bunnies, fingerprints, smudges, and other evidences of less-than-perfect housekeeping? Have you noticed too, the ever-advancing calendar brings to light all the untaught chapters, unwritten papers, and unmet academic goals -- all evidences of less-than-perfect homeschooling? There's something about fewer than forty days of school and standardized testing looming on the horizon that can send homeschooling mothers into what John Bunyan's Pilgrim called a "slough of despond."

I am the first to call homeschooling mothers to excellence. As children of the King, we should ascribe to a higher standard. We represent the Lord as well as homeschoolers everywhere, and should do everything "as though we were working for God, not for men." (Colossians 3:23).

I would like to call homeschooling mothers to another standard also, and this is the standard of grace. Grace knows any step toward a goal is progress, and doesn't condemn when the highest goal is yet unmet. Grace knows our hearts; hearts love the Lord and our families and earnestly want to be the best wife/mother/educator that we can be.

Should we strive for excellence? Absolutely. Will we always attain it? Absolutely not. As your school year draws to a close, my prayer is that you will finish well, with excellence and with grace. "This one thing I do, forgetting what is behind and straining toward what is ahead, I press on toward the goal to win the prize for which God has called me heavenward." (Philippians 3:13-14) Let's meet at the finish line!

Application Questions
1. What is the balance between striving for excellence and bestowing grace on yourself and others?
2. What does that look like from day to day?

Action Step for This Week

Remember that the homeschooling journey is a marathon, not a sprint, and every step toward the goal of educating your children is progress. Extend grace to yourself as you strive to finish the year with excellence.

Prayer of Commitment

Lord, help me to find the balance between my desire to homeschool with excellence and the reality that I sometimes fall far short of this goal. When necessary, help me extend grace to myself, my children, and those around me. Send me wisdom and insight to plan the last few months of school so we might finish this year well. More than anything else, enable our homeschool to glorify You.

DON'T DESPISE THE DAY OF SMALL THINGS

"Do not despise the day of small things."
Zechariah 4:10

Task Oriented. What comes to mind when you read these words? If you are deep into your second semester, checking off learning objectives and writing lesson plans, you might think of yourself as task oriented. Here is another word: Discouraged. Perhaps you are already discouraged as you work through the second half of your school year. Maybe discouragement won't happen until you are further into your homeschooling journey. If you are human, and especially if you are task oriented, discouragement will happen. When it does, it's important to know you are not alone.

The book of Zechariah was written to a task oriented, discouraged man. His name was Zerubbabel. He was the governor over post-exilic Jerusalem. This was the same Jerusalem that had been razed to the ground when Nebuchadnezzar swept through the land. Zerubbabel's task was to rebuild the temple. It was a big task. He had made a good start, but struggles from within and without discouraged the people and Zerubbabel, their governor.

As homeschoolers, you too face a big task. Sometimes struggles from within (disobedient children, learning challenges, health issues) and without (non-supportive parents, the pull of the world on our children, finances) discourage us and cause us to lose heart.

God cared that Zerubbabel was discouraged, and God cares if you are too. God sent the prophet Zechariah to speak words of encouragement. They apply to our lives as well.

First, God told Zerubbabel not to "despise the day of small things" (Zechariah 4:10). Zerubbabel had his eyes on the finished product, and the step by step, brick by brick, daily progress was slow, hard to measure, and sometimes disappointing. He wanted to see the temple, not the process.

God reminded Zerubbabel not to have his eyes so trained on the finish line that he missed the steps in the race. The message is clear for homeschooling parents. Sometimes we miss the small steps our children make because they haven't become the person/student/mature Christian we want them to be. "Do not despise the day of small things." Instead note the small things, write them down, and remark upon them to your children. Speaking as a parent of a graduate, the day will come when the temple is built, and it will have been built one brick at a time.

Second, God encouraged Zerubbabel with a reminder of how the task was to be accomplished, "Not by might, not by power, but by MY Spirit, says the Lord." (Zechariah 4:6) He confirmed that Zerubbabel, who was faithful from the first until the last, would see the day of rejoicing at the finished product -- a temple built to bring God glory. "What are you, O mighty mountain? (our seemingly "impossible" tasks) Before Zerubbabel (insert your name here) you will become level ground. Then he (Zerubbabel and US!) will bring out the capstone to shouts of "God bless it! God bless it!" (Zechariah 4:7)

Never forget, homeschooling mother, you have a part in building a temple that will bring God glory. God bless you as you homeschool in faith!

Application Question

What seems like a "mountain" in your homeschooling journey right now?

Action Step for This Week

List some "small things" that show progress in each of your children's lives right now. Commit to look intentionally for areas of progress in each child's life. Take the time to point these out to your children. Speak words of affirmation to him/her.

Prayer of Commitment

Lord, sometimes I get discouraged when I look at how far my children need to go before they "arrive." The progress seems so slow and messy. Sometimes it doesn't seem like progress at all. Thank you, Lord that You are doing a work in me and in my children through this adventure called homeschooling. Help me see little glimmers of hope along the way, and be quick to speak words of affirmation and encouragement into my children's ears as You speak words of encouragement into mine.

DO FEW THINGS, AND DO THEM WELL

"A nd whatever you do in word or deed, do all in the name of the Lord Jesus, giving thanks to God the Father through Him."
Colossians 3:17

"Do few things and do them well." I don't know how many years it has been since one of my homeschooling mentors spoke these timeless words at a homeschool support group meeting. They have rung in my ears ever since. I am tempted to simply share the quote without comment. The comment and its corresponding verse are that powerful. Sometimes, though, it is easier to examine our own lives through someone else's. I am willing to be that lens.

I asked myself today, "When was the last time I said, 'Take your time'?" When I die, I think they'll stamp my name on my tombstone as "Lori-Hurry-Up-Hatcher." When was the last time I didn't have to be somewhere or do something right now? When was the last time I allowed myself a cup of tea with a friend without planning it months in advance? When was the last time I sat with my Bible and my prayer journal and stopped when my "cup" was full instead of when the clock told me it was time to move on?

When was the last time we played a game, took a walk, or read an extra chapter in the family novel just because it was exciting, and we didn't want to stop? When was the last time we had a really good day of school instead of cutting every corner so we could rush out the door? When was the last time I didn't fall into bed exhausted, already overwhelmed with the tasks of the next day?

If your answers, like mine, fall short, it is time to reevaluate. Why did you begin to homeschool in the first place? What activities in your life are the most important? What is the best for your family and not just good? What have you sacrificed on the altar of busyness that you will regret when you look back?

We have our children for so short a season. Homeschooling takes time, lots of it, and it can't be done well from the driver's seat. Our marriages are gifts from God and need nurturing to thrive. Our souls need times of quiet and refreshing. Will you join me in reexamining whether we are doing "few things and doing them well?"

Application Questions
1. Why did you begin to homeschool in the first place?
2. What activities in your life are the most important?
3. What is the best for your family and not just good?
4. What have you sacrificed on the altar of busyness that you will regret when you look back?

Action Step for This Week

Take time to meet with your husband and ask yourselves the above questions. Commit to make the appropriate changes needed to bring your priorities back in order.

Prayer of Commitment

Lord, it is so easy to sacrifice the best on the altar of the good. Help us to seek Your face and Your will for our family. Give us insight to see the areas where we have gotten off track, become slaves to busyness, and committed to activities that are not a part of your perfect will for us. Help us acknowledge You in all our ways and trust You to direct our paths. (Proverbs 3:5-6)

FEBRUARY

THE PRIVILEGE OF TRAINING A CHILD

"These commandments that I give you today are to be on your hearts. Impress them on your children. Talk about them when you sit at home, when you walk along the road, when you lie down, and when you get up."
Deuteronomy 6:6-7

I recently had the privilege of caring for a friend's 5-year-old son. I work part-time as a dental hygienist, and just like it's good for me to physically sit in the chair every now and then to remind myself of how it feels to be a dental patient, caring for this kindergartener was a wonderful reminder of how it feels to parent a preschooler.

Parents of preschoolers, my hat is off to you! How quickly I had forgotten some of the interesting characteristics of five-year-olds: boundless energy, insatiable curiosity, and an uncanny ability to make a mess with everything they touch. Not to mention not sleeping very well at night (them and you), announcing loudly every time they have to go to the bathroom (even in church), and having an irrational fear of vegetables.

I had forgotten one universal quality that quickly became apparent after Seth's arrival into our household. I remembered that five-year-olds don't know how to think silently. Every thought that occurs to them must be spoken aloud. Since Seth didn't come from a Christian home, many of his thoughts were about our practices as Christians. "Why do you close your eyes when you pray?" "Why do you say, 'Amen'?" "Why do you thank God for our food when we get it from the grocery store?" "What's a Bible?" These were all questions my own children had asked, but somehow Seth's questions were especially exciting, because I realized I was watching him begin to understand there was a God in Heaven who cared about him and his family.

If you are a parent of a young child, or an older one for that matter, take heart. With each diaper you change and each runny nose you wipe, every mess you clean up and every Lego block you step on, you are earning the right to answer his questions. You are the privileged one who gets to teach her to fold her little hands to pray or watch while she drops her nickels and quarters into the offering plate each Sunday. You are there to hear him sing "God can do anything!" and whisper his prayers at bedtime.

These moments are worth every sacrifice you make. Not every child has a parent like you. Not every child knows from before he can speak that Jesus loves them. Not every child knows that God hears and answers prayers. Not every child knows that her mommy and daddy love God. Not every child knows what you know, and it is your privilege to teach them.

Application Questions

1. What are some of the characteristics of children you most enjoy?
2. Which characteristics challenge you the most?
3. What are you doing to prayerfully point your young ones to Christ?

Action Step for This Week

Think about what a great privilege it is to teach and train our children to love God. Commit to "be ready always to give an answer to every man that asks you a reason for the hope that lies within you, with meekness and fear." (I Peter 3:15) Apply this principle to your interaction with your children, intentionally looking for opportunities to point them to Christ during your day to day interactions.

Prayer of Commitment

Lord, thank You so much for the awesome privilege and responsibility You have given me to teach and train our children to know and love You. Help me never take this responsibility lightly, but be diligent and intentional about it. Keep me mindful of the fact that the days of my children's youth go by so quickly. Help me never wish those days away, but enjoy every minute, even the challenging ones. I know You as my heavenly parent provide the greatest example of patient parenting. Help me follow Your example as I parent my children with the strength and wisdom that comes from You.

March

TEACH THEM TO LOVE

"Be devoted to one another in brotherly love."
Romans 12:10

I know a family that has two brothers. One is outgoing and personable, the other is awkward and shy. Academically, one brother is brilliant, and the other is average. One brother has awards and honors that could line the most expansive room. The other brother has a trophy for "Most Improved" in 5th grade baseball and an Honorable Mention ribbon from a science fair.

These brothers are now both young adults. They attend the same university, and they love each other. Not only do they love each other, they enjoy each other. They voluntarily spend time together, unprompted by their parents.

It is the desire of all our hearts that we have children who love each other into and through adulthood, but sometimes we find ourselves at a loss to know how to cultivate sibling love.

Here are a few thoughts that will help you. First, allow no unkind words to be spoken in your home. Ephesians 4:29 tells us to "let no corrupt word come out of your mouth, but only that which is edifying" (or for the purpose of building others up.) If our children are to learn to love and appreciate each other, we must cultivate (and sometimes strongly enforce) the policy of affirmation and edification versus condemnation and ridicule. Children are not naturally kind. We must teach them. We must also employ the same policy when speaking to our children about what we require of them. This doesn't mean we don't correct them. It simply means every word we share with them is spoken in love (Ephesians 4:15).

Second, we must teach our children to rejoice and sorrow along with their siblings. They can share in the triumph of a job well done or a goal accomplished, and they can share in the sadness of a disappointing experience. (Romans 12:15) Make a point to have all the family attend baseball games, awards ceremonies, and school plays whenever possible. This becomes more difficult as families get older, but it is an amazing bonding experience when siblings share in one another's trials and triumphs.

Another way to help build relationships among our children is to encourage shared friends. Plan get-togethers with whole families, not just individual play dates. You may be surprised to find you have also developed some special friendships along the way.

Finally, speak words of vision into each of your children within each other's hearing. Rather than complain about their differences, you can embrace them. Never try to make one child fit into the other's mold. Say, "Johnny, you are such a good listener (instead of, "You are so quiet and shy.") Maybe one day you will be a counselor to help people with their problems."

The Lord did this as he commissioned Gideon in Judges 6:12. Instead of pointing out that Gideon was fearfully hiding from his enemies in the dark, He called him a "Mighty Warrior." God knew Gideon would one day become a brave leader.

God has created each of our children with special gifts and talents. It is our job to help recognize them, celebrate them, and draw them out. As we affirm their differences, our children hear our words of vision, embrace them for themselves, and learn to value the differences in their siblings that could otherwise be frustrating or challenging.

Love doesn't grow naturally. It must be cultivated. God bless you as you teach your children the second greatest commandment - to love one another!

Application Questions

1. Are your children characterized by a love for each other?
2. What can you do to help them appreciate their differences?
3. Are you modeling edification in your speech toward them or toward your husband?

Application Step for This Week

Purpose to carefully watch the words you say to your children and intentionally look for opportunities to build them up within each other's hearing.

Prayer of Commitment

Lord, it is my heart's desire to have a home that is characterized by love. I want my children to know they are loved and valued by both me and their siblings. Help me model kindness in my words and actions. Give me the patience to correct them when they are unkind. Help me see the potential in each of my children, and speak words of vision over them. Thank You for loving me and giving me the ability to demonstrate Your love in our family.

DISCOURAGEMENT – PART I

"Be strong and of good courage, fear not... for the LORD your God, He it is that goes with you; He will not fail you, nor forsake you."
Deuteronomy 31:6

Are homeschooling mothers more prone to discouragement than other moms? I don't know the answer, but I do know none of us are immune. Many moms, after being cooped up inside during a long winter, sometimes with sick children and several months of schooling ahead of them, often battle discouragement. Discouragement can weigh you down and rob you of your joy, motivation, and enthusiasm. It often paves the way for its cousin, depression, to set in.

The word "discourage" or "discouragement" appears only five times in the whole Bible. Does this mean discouragement is a twenty-first century phenomenon? Certainly not. David's psalms poignantly express his struggles with discouragement, and the Apostle Paul is a New Testament figure who shares how he "despaired even of life" in 2 Corinthians 1:8. Discouragement, like many other emotions, takes various forms and is therefore seldom summed up in a single word.

When we research discouragement in God's Word, we find several truths that help us battle discouragement.

The first occurrence of the word "discouraged" comes in Numbers 21:4. In the New International Version, the word is translated "impatient." I wonder, as homeschooling mothers how much of our discouragement comes because we become impatient with our children for not learning as quickly as we would like. Are fractions or multiplication tables taking forever? Will they ever learn to say please and thank you, and pick up their toys and clothes? Weighing heaviest on our hearts, when will they begin to show signs of spiritual life and vitality? How dearly we want all these things for our children. How impatient we get when they are not forthcoming.

Application Questions
1. How much of your discouragement can you trace back to impatience over some area of your child's development?
2. Are your expectations too high?
3. Are you discouraged as a result of comparing your children to someone else's?
4. Are you carrying the burden for something the Lord has to do in your child's life?

Action Step for This Week

Prayerfully seek God and ask Him to show you if impatience is at the root of your discouragement. If it is, surrender your timetable for your children to the Lord and ask Him to work in their lives to bring about growth and change in His perfect timing.

Prayer of Commitment

Lord, I confess that sometimes I get so frustrated and impatient with where my children are right now. Sometimes all I can see is how far they have to go and how slow their progress is. Help me see everything You have accomplished in and through our homeschooling. Give me patience and trust as I work alongside You to teach and train our children.

DISCOURAGEMENT – PART 2

" Be strong and of good courage, fear not... for the LORD your God, He it is that goes with you; He will not fail you, nor forsake you."
Deuteronomy 31:6

A second occurrence of the word "discouraged" is in connection with the report the spies brought back from the land of Canaan. While two spies were encouraging, the other ten were discouraging. They demoralized the Israelites with their words.

I challenge you to analyze the messages you are allowing to filter into your brain. Are they messages from women who have chosen a different educational option for their children and can't quite understand why you would think you could homeschool your children? These negative messages may be coming from a grandparent or someone else close to you who truly wants the best for your children, but doesn't feel that homeschooling is it.

If you and your husband have earnestly sought God's will for your children's education, ask God to give you peace and direction that this is His plan for your family. Then, like Joshua and Caleb, live in light of the fact that when God calls, He provides, equips, and blesses with rewards unimaginable. No one remembers the names of the other ten spies, but everyone knows Joshua and Caleb were men of faith who followed God regardless of what the "crowd" was saying or doing. Commit to be a Joshua or a Caleb today!

Application Question
Are you allowing critical words to overshadow the knowledge that God has called your family to homeschool?

Action Point for This Week

Begin a positive PR plan -- surround yourself with like-minded, positive homeschoolers. Invite one over for lunch. Find a homeschool support group and get involved. Make a list of why you are homeschooling, and post it in a prominent place.

Prayer of Commitment

Lord, sometimes I get discouraged and overwhelmed. Instead of focusing on what we are accomplishing in our homeschool, all I can see are the failures and inadequacies. Sometimes I doubt Your calling. Today Lord, I commit to trust Your work in our family and our homeschool. I pledge to thank You for the victories, both small and great, and trust You with everything that needs to be accomplished. I ask You to meet all of my children's needs, physically, spiritually, socially, and academically. Thank You for being our Provider.

WHAT DO YOU LIKE ABOUT HOMESCHOOLING?

"In everything give thanks, for this is the will of God in Christ Jesus concerning you!"
I Thessalonians. 5:13

What do you like about homeschooling? I asked my family this question recently, and the answers were a delightful reminder of the "perks" that go along with the awesome task of homeschooling our families.

We like homeschooling because…we have a teacher who loves us…we can stop and pray in the middle of class if we need to…we don't worry about anyone coming into our school and shooting us…if we don't understand something, our teacher helps us until we get it…we can eat and go to the bathroom whenever we need to…we don't have to ride a school bus…if a squirrel or a bird comes to the window, we can stop and study it for Science class…we get to read lots of great books…we get to go on cool field trips…we have a peer group that is like-minded and shares our values (this from Mom)…our dog gets to come to school with us…we don't have to get up so early in the morning…we can learn about God and not get arrested…we're always first in our class…our teacher teaches the Truth… we get to hug a lot.

What do you like about homeschooling? Take a few moments to ask yourself the question, and then ask your children. You'll be delightfully surprised at the answers!

Application Question

What are some of the benefits of the homeschooling lifestyle you often take for granted?

Action Step for This Week

Take time around the dinner table to talk about the things you and your children enjoy about homeschooling. Maybe even write them down. Stop and thank God for the privilege of homeschooling.

Prayer of Commitment

Lord, sometimes it's easy to focus on the things we don't like about the homeschooling lifestyle – the mountain of papers to grade, the house that never seems to stay clean, the lack of 'me' time. Help me this week to focus on the things I love about homeschooling. Help me lead my children to have a thankful heart about the privilege of homeschooling. Thank You for my husband, who works long hours so I can stay home and educate the children. Thank You that I live in a country where homeschooling is legal. Many families would love to home-school but can't for a variety of reasons. Help me never to take this opportunity for granted.

April

LOOK UP!

WHAT I LEARNED IN HOMESCHOOL

STONES OF REMEMBRANCE

HOW TO HAVE A HORRIBLE HOMESCHOOL DAY

LOOK UP!

"I lift my eyes to the hills, from where my help comes,"
Psalm 121:1

Although I have lived in the South for over thirty years, this was my first visit to the legendary Biltmore House, home of railroad magnate George W. Vanderbilt. Lured by my beauty-loving daughter to spend a few days in the mountains of North Carolina, we eagerly placed Biltmore House on the top of our "must see" list.

As we began our tour of the 19th century French mansion, I struggled to take in all the details of this beautiful home. Rich fabrics covered the walls, shining wood and marble floors stretched before us, and opulent furnishings told tales of the wealth and elegance of days gone by.

As we entered the Banquet Hall, a dining room modeled after an English Country manor house, my daughter exclaimed, "Look up!" Surrounding the room were at least fifteen massive animal heads gazing solemnly back at us. As I took in the china that graced the table, my daughter again directed my eyes skyward by pointing out the massive organ loft that housed a 1916 Skinner pipe organ big enough to fill my house. While I admired the paintings that graced the walls, my daughter once again pointed my eyes upward, discovering a detail I had missed -- the hall was ringed with flags from the original thirteen colonies, including one from my home state of Rhode Island with its message of HOPE. With a third reminder to "Look up," it was apparent to me that my daughter had a different way than I did of viewing this beautiful home.

Quietly, the Lord spoke to my heart. "Lori, as you move through life, how much do you miss by not looking up? More importantly, how often are you so focused on what is happening in front of you that you miss what is happening ABOVE you?"

With that gentle reminder, I realized how easy it is to become so involved and aware of our physical life here on earth that we miss what

God is doing in and around us. How often have I been overwhelmed with problems and concerns and totally missed the help and hope God offers me if I would just "look up?" God commanded Abraham to "lift up (his) eyes" to see the great inheritance God had promised him. (Genesis 13:14) Jesus himself encouraged and warned his disciples that when perilous times come, "Lift up your heads, because your redemption is drawing near." (Luke 21:28)

We would all do well to hear the message of Biltmore House and "Look up!"

Application Questions

1. Are you often so focused on the day-to-day challenges of running a homeschooling household that you lose sight of God's work going on around you?
2. Do problems and concerns cause you to seek God more or less?

Action Step for This Week

The next time you feel overwhelmed, take a few moments to sit quietly before the Lord and invite Him into your situation. Ask Him for wisdom, help, patience, and whatever else you need. Then watch to see how He answers your prayer.

Prayer of Commitment

Thank you, Lord, that Your Word is full of promises I can claim. Help me to remember to "lift my eyes" to see the rich provision available to me if I would simply ask. Make me aware of the spiritual events taking place right in front of me in the seemingly insignificant details of our homeschooling day and use my example to teach my children what it means to seek You for everything.

WHAT I LEARNED IN HOMESCHOOL

" B eing confident of this, that He who began a good work in you will be
faithful to complete it."
Philippians 1:6

When my husband and I made the decision to homeschool our first-born daughter, we knew it was a noble, good, and unselfish choice. We knew it was the best option to help her reach her full potential. What I didn't realize was that the decision to homeschool her would also help me reach my full potential. This is what I learned in homeschool.

I learned the difference between toads and frogs, butterflies and moths, prepositions and verb clauses, and Virginia Creeper and Poison Ivy. I learned how gold is mined, to name all 50 states and capitals, and that the Second Law of Thermodynamics specifically applies to homeschooling households. I learned to write more legibly (italics), and I learned the names of my congressmen. They learned mine as I began to speak out on behalf of homeschoolers in our state and across our nation.

I learned to trust God to provide finances, resources, SAT tutors, musical instruments and teachers, as well as patience, kindness, and self-control. I learned to pray instead of cry (usually), learned to set a hard subject aside for a few weeks and try again later, and to write for publication as I was teaching my small ones to communicate through the written word. I learned about classical music and art history, stoichiometry and balanced equations, and that it was not against health department rules to have a sheep's eyeball next to the milk in my refrigerator.

I discovered that while I was teaching my daughter, I, too, was learning, growing, stretching, and maturing. I, too, was becoming the woman God wanted me to be. I learned to thank my daughter and the Lord for the finest education love can buy. On May 19, 2007 she graduated with honors from our homeschool, and I returned to the ninth grade for the third time. After all, I had yet to master Algebra!

Application Questions
1. What were your initial reasons for homeschooling your children?
2. Have they changed over the years?
3. What have been some unexpected benefits you have received through homeschooling?
4. Have you unearthed or resurrected any talents of your own that surprise you?

Action Steps for This Week

Take time to list some of the things you have learned through homeschooling, and thank the Lord for them.

Prayer of Commitment

Lord, so often it is the case that You bless us in ways we never imagine when we choose to obey You. Thank You for the rich blessings you have brought into our family's life and into my life personally through our decision to homeschool. I recognize You are using this homeschooling adventure to refine me, teach me more about Yourself, and grow my faith. You are teaching me skills I might never have learned, bringing friends into my life I might never have met, and filling my life with good things. Help me count these blessings when I am tempted to grumble and complain.

STONES OF REMEMBRANCE

"O God, we have heard with our ears, our fathers have told us the work that you did in their days, in the days of old..."
Psalm 44:1

Children love stories. Everyone loves stories. I suspect that was why Jesus chose to wrap many of his important lessons in stories. In the age of instant everything and fifteen-second sound bites, I fear we parents are losing our ability to tell stories. I'm not talking about "Handsome Prince stories," as my starry-eyed girls would call them, or even "Big Ugly Monster stories," like some of their Boy Scout friends preferred, but faith stories like the ones in the Old Testament. Not only does the Bible command us to tell our children faith stories, but it goes one step further. God tells us to use visuals.

Remember when God parted the Jordan River and allowed the children of Israel to walk across on dry ground into the Promised Land? The first thing God commanded his children to do after they reached the other side was to set up "stones of remembrance." He instructed them to take twelve stones out of the Jordan River and construct a memorial. Its purpose? "... So that this will be a sign among you. In the future, when your children ask you, 'What do these stones mean to you?' you should tell them, 'The waters of the Jordan were cut off in front of the ark of the Lord's covenant...' Therefore these stones will always be a memorial." (Joshua 4:6-7)

Our family has applied this principle through the use of a Memorial Box. It is a shadow box with compartments and a glass front. Within the box, we have placed carefully chosen items that represent significant faith stories from our family's history.

One of the most precious items in our box is a stone, similar to the Children of Israel's stones, that was once part of a wall in our neighborhood. It is special to us because my husband was sitting on this wall when an encyclopedia saleswoman came down the road asked him, "Would you like to hear about how to have a relationship with Jesus?" He said "Yes," and his life was changed forever.

Other items in the box include a tiny computer to represent the computer God sent our way when we had no money to purchase one, a key chain from the job God provided for my husband after two months of unemployment, and a receipt marked "Paid in Full" that represents the hospital bill that mysteriously disappeared before we could make the first payment.

There is no magic in the box or in the stories that come from it. The power is in what these stories represent. Faith stories testify of a God who loves us, who cares and provides for us, and who hears our prayers. Faith is contagious! When your children hear the stories of how God has been faithful to you, they will begin to believe He will be faithful to them as well. Faith stories, with visual aids, are marvelous tools for preserving the history of God's faithfulness to your family. They are also powerful witnesses to those who will visit your home. "Daddy, what's that rock doing in our Memorial Box?" "Well sweetie, let me tell you a story..."

I hope you will begin your own family's Memorial Box today. It will take a lifetime to complete.

Application Questions

1. What are some of your family's unique faith stories?
2. How do they demonstrate God's faithfulness to your family through the years?
3. What objects can you gather to represent each faith story?

Action Step for This Week

At the dinner table this week, begin to share some of your family's faith stories. Pair each story with an object to represent it, and begin your Memorial Box. When others visit, share your stories.

Prayer of Commitment

Lord, You have been so faithful to our family. Help us never forget all You have done for us. Help us preserve the legacy of Your faithfulness for our children and future generations through a Memorial Box or some other means. May we use it as a powerful testimony of Your protection, provision, and blessing upon us.

APRIL

HOW TO HAVE A HORRIBLE HOMESCHOOL DAY

"For I always do those things that please Him."
John 8:29

If the children handed you your inhaler the last time you laughed because they mistook the sound for an asthma attack, this devotion is for you. If you consider running to the grocery store "exercise," keep reading. If the children are climbing the laundry pile and calling it Mt. Everest, and you record it on your lesson plan as a field trip, don't skip this one.

If homeschooling has been going smoothly lately, and you're accomplishing everything on your lesson plan, the kids are polite, kind, and well-behaved, and you're so far ahead with household chores you've begun taking in laundry, look up "satire" in the dictionary and read how to have a horrible homeschool day.

1. Skip your quiet time with the Lord because you have entirely too much to do today. That nonsense about God honoring the time you spend with Him first HAS to be an urban legend.

2. Wait until dinner time to decide what you're having for dinner. Those ladies who meal plan, or even just decide by 10 am what they plan to fix for supper are so, well, structured. Imagine the idea of having a whole meal in the crock pot early in the day! Who would want to smell savory beef stew or minestrone soup all day long? It's enough to give you indigestion!

3. Wait until Sunday night (or Monday morning) to lesson plan for the week. It adds to spontaneity (and ulcers). Never mind that it wastes the kids' best energy while they wait for mom to come up with SOMETHING for them to do. Who wants to take an hour or two out of a weekend simply because it will help the whole next week go smoother and save time and energy later? Whatever happened to living on the edge?

4. Don't take time out to exercise. This is guaranteed to cost you in the long run. Why, thirty minutes walking the dog or working out on the treadmill might give you more energy to get stuff done, and who wants to

do MORE STUFF?!

 5. Never take a break. No twenty minute power nap while the kids are reading or playing in their rooms. No mandatory quiet time for all mid-way through the day. No sit-down lunches; just eat on your feet between subjects. Just because everything, from electronics, to puppies, to God stops now and then doesn't mean you should. These rules don't apply to mothers.

 6. Never take time to play and laugh with your kids. Everyone knows homeschooling is serious business. It is NOT a laughing matter!

Application Questions
1. When things get busy, what is the first discipline that falls by the wayside?
2. What would be some measurable benefits to planning ahead?
3. What personal habit would you like to work toward? Laughing more? Getting regular physical and spiritual rest?

Action Step for This Week
 Chose one of the areas mentioned above and purpose to approach it differently. Evaluate at the end of the week and tweak your plan if necessary.

Prayer of Commitment
 Lord, You were a busy man when You walked this earth, but You still found time to spend with God, laugh and eat with Your family and friends, and rest. Today's scripture tells us You always did those things that pleased Your Father. I suspect God told You each morning during Your quiet time how to do that. More than anything, I want our homeschool and our family to glorify You. Help me to sit at Your feet and let You order my day.

May

STANDING IN THE SHADOW

CHOOSING THAT WHICH IS BETTER

RUNNING THE RACE

THANK YOU

STANDING IN THE SHADOW

"I praise you because I am fearfully and wonderfully made; your works are wonderful."
Psalm 139:14

Our Sunday school class was enjoying a fun afternoon of family bowling. Between turns, I took the opportunity to "size up" the competition. I watched several interesting scenarios play out as the afternoon progressed.

In my lane, I watched a young man bowl a very respectable score. I knew his older brother played on the local high school bowling team. "I didn't know Jake bowled," I commented to his mother. "Oh, he usually doesn't bowl, because he never bowls as well as his brother." What a joy to watch the young man's beaming smile as he scored more than a few spares and strikes.

Two lanes over, I watched another story unfold. One man, a relative newcomer to our class, was bowling up a storm. This man earned the high score in his lane and came close to having the overall high score of the day. Later I found out it was the first time he had bowled. He loved it!

We can draw some homeschool conclusions from these scenarios. As you make choices for your school year, ask yourself a few questions. Does one of my children often stand in the shadow of another? This may be because of age, birth order, personality, intelligence, or natural ability. If so, seek out an atmosphere or activity that will allow your child to experience success and to shine. Explore different activities than those in which his sibling may be especially skillful. Allow him to try a different sport, musical instrument, or hobby. On the flip side, don't require him to continue an activity in which he has no real hope of success just because his other siblings are doing it. Allow him the freedom to be different.

Our second scenario raises another point. Do you have a timid child, one who is not very adventurous and prefers to "play it safe? She might hesitate to take chances because she might fail. If this is the case, I encourage you to help her broaden her horizons. Perhaps she has shown some swimming ability, but the thought of swim team is intimidating. Make a deal with her, "Try it for a month. If you don't like it, you can quit." Then you've given her an out if it really isn't right for her, yet you've encouraged her to try.

Another approach is to keep your ears tuned to opportunities, field trips, etc., that you think might match his interests, and sign him up. The key to this is to be sure the subject is at least remotely interesting to them, not just you. Giving him the opportunity to safely explore a potential area of interest may expose him to a field, hobby, sport, or ministry in which he finds he is very gifted. Who knows, one day he might say, "I wouldn't be here today if my mom hadn't encouraged me to give it a try!"

Application Questions

1. Do you have a child who tends to stay in the shadow of a more outgoing or gifted child?
2. What might this child's less obvious but equally special abilities be?
3. How can you encourage him/her to try something new?

Action Step for the Week

Pray and ask God to show you how you can help your shy or hesitant child to blossom.

Prayer of Commitment

Lord, while I was reading this devotional, you brought _____ to mind. Help me know how to encourage him/her to reach his/her full potential. I know You have gifted this child in a unique and special way, but sometimes he is overshadowed by his sibling(s). Give me wisdom to see just how to help him to realize Your special plan for his life.

CHOOSING THAT WHICH IS BETTER

"Martha, Martha," the Lord answered, 'You are worried and upset about many things, but only one thing is needed. Mary has chosen what is better, and it will not be taken away from her.'"

Luke 10:41-42

Winston, our red-headed freckled-faced four-legged child was rescued from the Anderson Animal Shelter almost a year ago. Like so many rescued animals, Winston has a healthy appreciation for all things good and takes nothing for granted. He loves everyone, but according to my family, Winston loves me best.

Like my children when they were toddlers, Winston follows me everywhere. If I move to the kitchen to answer the phone, he follows me. If I go to the laundry room to drop another load of clothes into the washer, he follows me there. And, like my toddlers once did, he even follows me to the bathroom.

Why does Winston follow me everywhere? It's not because I have a pocket full of treats to dole out to him at regular intervals. It's not because he wants me to toss his football or hold one side of his tug toy. Winston really doesn't want anything when he follows me around. He follows me around because he loves me and simply wants to be in my presence.

In the Gospel of Luke, Jesus reprimanded Martha, ". . . you are concerned about so many things . . . but Mary has chosen the best." Martha had been busy for days doing good things to make Jesus' visit special, but when Jesus arrived, she was so busy doing good things she missed the best thing of all -- sitting at Jesus' feet. Martha loved Jesus, but she loved a clean house, well-prepared food, and matching table linens more. According to the Savior, she had traded what was good for what was best.

Mary, on the other hand, had worked just as hard as Martha prior to Jesus' visit, but when it was time to sit at His feet and enjoy Him, she did. And she was richer for it. She was commended for all eternity by her Lord.

Hard working, conscientious homeschooling mother, don't immerse yourself in the good and miss the best. Work hard teaching and training your children, keep a neat and orderly house, volunteer at church, and help your neighbors, but make sure you begin each day with a time to sit at Jesus' feet and simply be in His presence. Not asking for things or expecting anything, just being in His presence.

God will honor you as you put Him first in your day. I remember a conversation with a dear friend who said, "I missed my quiet time today, and it was downhill all day long. I don't know if having a quiet time today would have changed anything about my circumstances, but I know I would have handled things a lot better." Any time you invest in your relationship with the Lord will be returned to you in other ways. Spend some time at Jesus feet today. After all, you love Him best.

Application Questions
1. What are you worried and upset about?
2. What "good thing" tends to distract you from spending time with God each day?
3. Are you willing to mentally set those things aside today and focus on the relationship with the One you love best?

Action Step for This Week
Just like you would a doctor's appointment or a lunch date, schedule in a time to sit at Jesus' feet today.

Prayer of Commitment
Lord, I confess I am often overwhelmed by the many tasks that fill my day. They all seem so urgent and important. More than anything else though, I want to choose what is best, and that is to spend time with You. Help me set aside time every day to sit at Your feet.

RUNNING THE RACE

"Let us run with perseverance the race that is set before us, looking unto Jesus, the Author and Finisher of our faith."
Hebrews 12:2

During my sophomore year in high school, I tried out for track. As I trained with the team, it became apparent that I was a "flash" – someone who started out bright and hot and faded quickly. My coach decided I was perfectly suited for running hurdles. Until that day, I had never seen a set of hurdles, let alone run them! Running hurdles, like any other skill, can be learned, so I began to train.

First I learned how to place my feet in the starting blocks when the starter called out, "Runners take your mark." I learned to raise my body up in preparation to launch when the starter said, "Set," and how to blast out of the blocks when the gun fired.

Next I learned I had to match my stride with the amount of distance between the starting block, first hurdle, and the subsequent nine hurdles that followed. When an athlete runs, going over the hurdle should be just another stride. There should be no change in her pace, and her stride should carry her over the hurdle with no extra effort. One-two-three-hurdle. One-two-three-hurdle. One-two-three-hurdle.

I soon learned that too long or too short a stride, a stumble as I ran, or not enough steps between hurdles meant instead of "running" the hurdles, I did what no self-respecting hurdler ever wanted to do, and that was to "bunny hop." A stride is forward motion. A bunny hop is vertical motion. Needless to say, if I had vertical motion, I was not heading forward.

During my first track meet, I faltered in my stride and my left knee crashed into the hurdle. It broke my forward stride, threw my count off, and I bunny hopped over the remaining nine hurdles in humiliation. The next day in practice, guess what the coach had me working on? Getting my left knee up so I could clear the hurdles and keep my stride.

What does this have to do with homeschooling? When I first began running track, I thought the hurdles were the key to running. I quickly found out it wasn't the occasional hurdle that mattered, but how I ran the track in between. Was I steady and consistent? Did I plan my course and work my plan? Did I keep my eye on the finish line, or did I get distracted?

Homeschooling mom, it is not the occasional hurdle that determines our homeschooling success, but instead it is the straight and narrow path we run with perseverance between life's hurdles.

There was nothing glorious about running that sandy dirt track day in and day out, but on race days, when the hurdles were out, the consistency and character I learned between the hurdles carried me over and beyond them to win the race. The consistency and character you are building into your children day after day on the "dirt track" of homeschooling is what will equip them to clear the hurdles in their lives without breaking their stride.

Application Questions

1. Why is it easy to lose sight of the finish line when you are slogging through the day to day routine of homeschooling?
2. How can the daily disciplines you build into our children carry them through the rough patches of life?
3. Think about the phrase, "Practice makes permanent." What permanent practices do you want to instill in yourself and your children?

Action Point for This Week

Evaluate the daily disciplines of your days to ensure your children are practicing what you want to become permanent.

Prayer of Commitment

Lord, you are so faithful to instruct us how to run the race with perseverance. Thank You that as You coach me, I can in turn coach my children. Help me keep my eyes on the finish line so that I might experience the joy of hearing You say, "Well done, good and faithful servant!"

THANK YOU

"We give thanks to God and the Father of our Lord Jesus Christ, praying always for you"
Colossians 1:3

THANK YOU for teaching your child to love and study God's Word. He may be my pastor one day.

THANK YOU for teaching your child to dissect that yucky cow's heart on your kitchen table. Her hands may hold the scalpel that will one day save my life.

THANK YOU for teaching your child to work hard, pick up his clothes, be kind to children, and kiss his mother goodnight. He may one day be the father of my grandchildren.

THANK YOU for teaching your child to love learning. She may one day research the cure for the cancer that threatens us all.

THANK YOU for teaching your child that all life is precious. He may one day sign the legislation that protects me when I am old, senile, or no longer productive.

THANK YOU for teaching your child to pray. She may one day help bring about revival in my generation.

THANK YOU for teaching your child to love people and peace. He may one day broker a peace agreement that prevents war in my lifetime.

THANK YOU for teaching your child to share her faith. She may one day be the Sunday school teacher who leads my grandchildren to the Lord.

THANK YOU for another year of homeschooling. Well done.

"And let us not be weary in well doing, for in due season we shall reap, if we do not faint."
Galatians 6:9

For more words of encouragement and inspiration, please visit Lori's blog at **http://www.lori-benotweary.blogspot.com**.

SIX REASONS
HOMESCHOOLING MOMS QUIT
...AND HOW YOU CAN AVOID THEM

As a leader in the homeschool community for over ten years and a 17-year homeschooling veteran, I have had the privilege of interacting with hundreds of homeschooling mothers. While most begin well, many quit after several months or years of unsuccessful homeschooling. I believe there are several reasons why homeschool moms quit. I share them with you in the form of six questions:

1. Is Your Homeschool Dedicated?

Many couples begin homeschooling simply because it seems to be the best educational option for their children. They may have had a bad experience with a public school, can't afford a private one, or live in an area with few options. Maybe they know someone who homeschools or are feeling pressure from others at church to "try it." It is no surprise then, at the first sign of difficulty, they entertain thoughts of quitting.

While any one of the above reasons to homeschool is not wrong, the missing component in this list is the element of God's will for the education for your children. There are times when homeschooling is joyous, satisfying, and successful. There are other times when it is challenging, frustrating, and seems to be failing. If you do not have clear calling and direction from God to homeschool your children, you will not have that calling to fall back on when times get hard.

We encountered difficulty when one of our daughters reached eighth grade. Convinced she was missing something vital by not attending the local public school in our neighborhood, she mounted an all out frontal attack on our decision to homeschool her. While she made some convincing arguments that my husband and I considered out of respect to her, what led us to continue to homeschool was the knowledge that God had called us to homeschool. The reasons we continue to homeschool had not changed.

We were led to homeschool in order that we might disciple our daughters, not just educate them. We were led to homeschool our girls in order to have the flexibility to explore opportunities linked to their unique giftedness without being locked into a school day or calendar. We were led to homeschool so they might have focused, one-on-one instruction specifically tailored to their needs and abilities. We were led to homeschool so we, their parents, would be making the final decisions concerning what they learned.

God had led us to these reasons, and they had not changed. Therefore, His calling to homeschool our children had not changed. While any major decision requires a step of faith, taking the time to seek God's will through prayer, Bible reading, circumstances, and the godly counsel of others will enable you to have a strong foundation for the reasons you homeschool. This will be an anchor when the winds of circumstance blow against your commitment and cause you to want to quit.

Note: I am in no way implying that someone who stops homeschooling mid-way is out of God's will. There are several valid reasons why parents might need to seek another educational option for their children. I am only encouraging you to seek God's will for your family and commit your way to Him in order to have a sure calling that will help you to weather the challenging times.

2. Are You Disconnected?

Many homeschooling moms quit because they are lonely and disconnected. They face day after day at home with no adult interaction. They miss the companionship of other adults and put undue stress on their relationship with their husbands because they expect them to meet all their needs for conversation and companionship. Their children are lonely too, and seldom have the opportunity to play with other children.

Human beings are social creatures. Even in the perfect relationship Adam had with God in the garden, God said, "It is not good for man to be alone," and He created Eve. The same principle of aloneness applies to us. While your primary relationship needs should be met within your relationship with the Lord and with your family, you need others to challenge, encourage, and enrich your life.

Scripture is replete with examples of the value of Christian friendship and companionship. One of my favorite examples is the beautiful friendship between David and Jonathan. They worked, played, and worshipped together. "As iron sharpens iron, so one man sharpens another." (Proverbs 27:17)

If you are contemplating quitting because you are lonely and disconnected, DON'T. Instead, do everything you can to find a support network of other homeschooling moms. Search the Internet for homeschool support groups or organizations in your area. Attend a support group meeting, visit different groups, frequent places where homeschoolers go. If you see a mom with children at the library, grocery store, park, or museum during the day, you can usually assume they are homeschooling too. Take the initiative to introduce yourself and your children. I have made lifelong friends by being the first to reach out. Don't give up if your efforts don't produce results immediately. Even if you are extremely isolated due to geography or other life circumstances, avail yourself of online homeschool forums. They network homeschooling moms and children all over the world.

Most important of all, PRAY and ask God to direct you to other homeschooling families. Ask Him for a special friend for each of your children. Don't homeschool alone. The benefits of doing life together are worth working for! For additional insight, read the devotional "Don't Struggle Alone" on page 48.

3. Are Your Children Disciplined?

Many homeschooling moms quit because their children won't obey them. I cannot overemphasize the necessity of establishing the discipline of obedience in your home. If your children do not obey you in the basic areas of life, they will not obey you when you tell them to complete their multiplication tables or write their spelling words.

I have seen bright, intelligent, talented mothers, who in their before-children days held positions of authority in the business world, reduced to screaming, begging, powerless victims of the tiny tyrants that live in their homes. It is a tragic sight.

I don't have the time or space here to address this issue at length, but I will say you are doing your children a great disservice and sabotaging your ability to homeschool successfully if you and your husband don't establish yourselves as the authorities in your home. As you teach your children to respect and submit to your authority, you are teaching them to respect and submit to God. Scripture tells us not to withhold correction from a child, (Proverbs 23:13) and to discipline him "while there is hope." As we teach our children self-discipline, we build into them the ability to succeed in life. "Whoever has no rule over his own spirit is like a city broken down, without walls."(Proverbs 25:28)

Many of us grew up in dysfunctional, non-Christian homes and did not have the benefit of seeing godly parenting modeled. If this is your story, you will have to be much more intentional about finding a mentor. Seek out a godly older woman with well-behaved children and pick her brain. Ask her if you and your husband can meet with her and her husband on a regular basis. If this is not an option, there are many excellent books written on this subject. One of my favorites is John Rosemond's *Parenting by the Book* (Howard House 2007). More than just about anything else, undisciplined, disobedient children will ruin your chances to homeschool successfully.

4. Are You Discouraged?

Many homeschooling moms quit because they are discouraged. They have come to me over the years to confess, "I am so discouraged. I want to quit." If you feel this way, take heart. You are not alone. Everyone feels discouraged at one time or another. You are most vulnerable to discouragement when you are tired, sick, or stressed. These factors make it much easier for your emotions to overwhelm you and cause you to think irrationally. Purpose, during a time when homeschooling is going well, that you will never make a decision about homeschooling when you are sick, tired, or stressed. Ask your husband or friend to hold you to that commitment.

The most important things to remember when you are discouraged and feel like quitting is that you are not alone, and you are not unspiritual for feeling that way. Godly men like Elijah and David struggled with discouragement, and its cousin, depression. For help in knowing how to deal with discouragement, please read the devotionals on page 87 and 89 of this book, Discouragement, parts 1 & 2.

5. Are You Having Doubts?

Many homeschooling moms quit because of doubts. They wonder if they are single-handedly sabotaging their children's entire academic future. They wonder if they have chosen the right curriculum, enrolled their children in the right extra-curricular activities, and are using the right Bible study materials. When they encounter difficulties, they wonder if their children need a "real" teacher. Surely if they were in school, they reason, their children wouldn't be having these struggles. Stormie O'Martian, in her book *The Power of Praying for Your Adult Children* (Harvest House 2009) says there are only two ways to avoid guilt as a parent. I believe these ways are equally applicable to the demon of doubt in homeschooling. "The first (way to avoid guilt) is to die soon after your child is born. The second is to walk with God every day, and ask Him for wisdom about everything" (17).

Doubts are normal, and in their proper place can cause you to reevaluate areas and decisions that might need adjustment. Doubts cause you to seek God's face, His power, and His wisdom with an urgency unfelt by those who are self-confident. Doubt can be a good thing if dealt with constructively. Doubt given over to the Lord can cause you to be stronger, more confident, and more obedient as you rest in HIS strength and not your own.

6. Have You Tapped into the Divine?

Many homeschooling moms quit because they say they just can't do it anymore. They have reached the end of their strength, joy, and desire. I tell them, "Congratulations, now you can really begin to homeschool."

In the early days of our homeschooling journey, I was very naïve. I assumed because I had navigated my own education successfully, I was at least reasonably qualified to educate my own children. It took me about 6 months of kindergarten to realize that ability and conscientiousness did not a homeschool make. One day when both I and my daughter were in tears over phonics and her inability to read, I learned the most valuable lesson of all about homeschooling – I cannot do it in my own strength.

I am frail, sinful, and selfish. I have blind spots and inadequacies. I stink at Algebra, and Chemistry equations make me break out in a cold sweat. I'd rather stay in bed than get up and have my quiet time, and I'd rather eat ice cream than carrot sticks. I have baggage from my own childhood that impacts the way I interact with my children, and I struggle daily to submit to my husband. I'd rather read a fluffy novel than Dickens' Great Expectations.

There is nothing within myself that would enable me to succeed at the monumental task of homeschooling, but I have. Through no ability of my own, I have home educated two precious daughters through elementary, middle and high school. One has graduated from college Magna cum Laude and the other is just beginning her college journey.

Through it all, as I have sought God's face and asked him for strength, wisdom, insight, and provision, He has been faithful. I want to leave you with one of my favorite Bible passages. May you claim it as your own as you press forward in faith to accomplish great things for God in and through your homeschool.

"But we have this treasure in earthen vessels, that the excellence of the power may be of God and not of us. We are hard pressed on every side, yet not crushed; we are perplexed, but not in despair; persecuted, but not forsaken; struck down, but not destroyed-- always carrying about in the body the dying of the Lord Jesus, that the life of Jesus also may be manifested in our body... Therefore we do not lose heart. Even though our outward man is perishing, yet the inward man is being renewed day by day. For our light affliction, which is but for a moment, is working for us a far more exceeding and eternal weight of glory, while we do not look at the things which are seen, but at the things which are not seen. For the things which are seen are temporary, but the things which are not seen are eternal." (2 Corinthians 4:4-10, 16-18)

God bless you as you homeschool your children in faith!
                    -Lori